Once to Every Man

Once to Every Man

A Novel

Elizabeth Cain

iUniverse, Inc.
Bloomington

Once to Every Man
A Novel

This is a work of fiction. All of the characters, names, incidents, organizations, and dialogue in this novel are either the products of the author's imagination or are used fictitiously.

iUniverse books may be ordered through booksellers or by contacting:

iUniverse
1663 Liberty Drive
Bloomington, IN 47403
www.iuniverse.com
1-800-Authors (1-800-288-4677)

ISBN: 978-1-4759-3246-1 (sc)
ISBN: 978-1-4759-3247-8 (hc)
ISBN: 978-1-4759-3248-5 (e)

Library of Congress Control Number: 2012910363

Printed in the United States of America

iUniverse rev. date: 08/08/2012

Dedicated to my husband, Jerome, who believed in me when I first told him the story in 1962, and is still with me in 2012 as the characters have taken on a life of their own. Because of his patience and his encouragement, the protagonists of my dream have a voice at last.

Author's Note

✧ ✦ ✧

This work is fiction. The characters are not based on the relationships or identities of any persons living or dead. However, it is set in a time and place that warrants some historical background.

The events occur between 1953 and 1985 in East Africa, England, and the United States. The fifties and sixties were turbulent times in Tanganyika, where the story begins. There was much tribal conflict, shifting of loyalties, and a deep resentment of British authority and white people in general. In 1961, the British rulers were rejected from the country, although in a somewhat more peaceful manner than presented here. In 1964, Tanganyika became known as Tanzania.

In Africa, a few villages are called by a Swahili name significant to the theme. The geographical locations and descriptions are not always to scale. Translations of Swahili words are noted on the last page.

Amani to all who read, all who take the characters and Africa into their hearts.

Once to every man and nation
Comes the moment to decide,
In the strife of truth with falsehood,
For the good or evil side;
Some great cause, God's new Messiah,
Offering each the bloom or blight,
And the choice goes on forever
Twixt that darkness and the light …

—James Russell Lowell, 1884

White

✧ ✦ ✧

I knew at dawn that Huzuni was crumbling at last under seasons of war. I rose with the coming light and rushed out along the shadowy paths of the village, restraining a cry. The straw-yellow huts still huddled in the dusty clearing, fat earthen pots rested in their dark doorways, and scattered fires smoldered in their shallow pits. The village remained. And yet, it had gone from its accustomed place in the serenity of tribal life to this new and inharmonious break of day.

A dim horizon surged through curtains of flaming orange, its stark silhouette black instead of green, burned and charred against the scarlet sky. The heat spiraled ominously from earth to treetops to high winds, although the sun was yet an hour away. The sleepers did not wake with soft laughter or the cheerful clanging of pans. The livestock did not clamor for their feed or morning trek to the water hole. They turned, almost soundlessly, pacing, then waiting, pacing, then waiting. The birds did not sing their familiar greeting to the day but called fearfully from nest to nest with hoarse cries and confused flapping of their wings. The whole forest seemed alive … with death.

Odd—to think of life and death in the same moment. But that was the way it had always been. We struggled from day to day with forces and dreams we didn't understand and were never ready for the change from light to dark … or the heartbreak.

I waited in that place between life and death on the edge of an isolated village in the green hills of the great continent of Africa. It was my fourth summer in the land, a land that was constantly changing. The people that had known peace now faced restlessness and fear, things beyond their tribal world, faces that were not black. I had one of those faces. I had come with books and prayers and dreams for them that were not their dreams. Others came to destroy their dreams, stayed long enough to leave their senseless imprint on the land, and went away again. Some of us stayed … to heal the wounds, to give hope to those who might still trust the words of strangers.

And yet, I was no stranger in the valley of Huzuni, no less guilty for my part in the upheaval of their old ways, their old beliefs, their acceptance of a white woman's tale of blood and redemption of sin, for which they had no name. I, at least, did not tell them lies, did not exploit their childlike faith, did not deceive them for my own sake. Not until today.

But today there were only a handful of natives in the little valley—eight men, thirteen women, and a half-dozen children. They had been afraid to go, and perhaps a few of them too loyal to betray the Master I served and whom they served because of me. A handful for me to love. A handful for me to betray.

There had been more at one time, many more, in this sanctuary called Huzuni, so named after the misery of Christ by some founding missionary long ago, where slowly, suspiciously, black men accepted the end of misery through Him. But they were no longer lured by gifts of medicine or trinkets or tools to visit the white missionary, to listen to her strange, sad story of the One who bore nails in His hands and feet. When it came time to choose sides, color was stronger than creed. One by one, the villagers slipped away, taking food and drugs and clothing. Not one Bible was missing. Even that, the taking of one Bible, would have given me hope. But the Gospel here would die, as surely as those few black believers, whom I must leave in the end.

"Helicopters will come and rescue us!" That is what I told my people, my wary-eyed brothers and sisters in Christ. "We will be safe," I said. But I knew they would send only one of the flying machines. "Let the blacks take care of the blacks," they would say. And the evacuation of one would begin.

I scanned the sky. An hour had passed. A martial eagle sailed by overhead and disappeared into the tangled growth that surrounded us. He seemed forlorn and lost, another homeless creature seeking a safe place. The rising sun blinded me to his flight and to all the secret watchers from the green and to every trusting black at my side. And that is when the drums began ... and the running feet ...

I prayed in the streets of my African home, kneeling in the dirt where pagan feet had fled. And the answer came, faintly at first and then frighteningly loud and real. I was certain now, there was only one! One silver helicopter hovering in the stark sky. I could almost hear the emotionless chatter of the copilot: "British Air Patrol to base, in the air over Huzuni, preparing to set down ... only one person visible, female, Caucasian ... may be hurt or under attack ... going in to attempt rescue ... over."

The copter whirled ever near, swift and powerful and bright. I looked for those shining black faces for whom I had suffered and with whom I had rejoiced, those few who had not abandoned me. Why should I be spared, if not these helpless few? They were my reason for being here after all, and if I were now lifted up, freed from their questioning eyes, from their questionable fate, I could never return. I could never speak the name of the Lord to them again, nor to anyone who knew what I had done.

I ran back toward the village. I did not look at the chopper careening earthward. The children were hurrying out now, when they saw me there. They were twirling with bare black feet and laughing eyes and pointing at the sky. "See! See! *Eropleni!* Angel with swift wings! Our Father has sent him, and we shall go up with Him and not be afraid anymore!" And I had only one prayer left. *Please God, show them your face in the end* ... But the drums crashed into my prayer, louder, closer, more final. And then they were silenced by the thrashing whir of the giant blades in the morning air.

✛   ✛   ✛

The first thing I saw was a man carrying three cameras and a large notepad. He was rushing toward me, bent over under the force of the whirling rotors. He was trying to tell me something, but the noise devoured his words and only his lips moved as he staggered upon me. I began to back away from him, but he called my name.

"Miss Pavane!" he shouted, moving with me.

He knew who I was!

"Jim Stone ... *London Free Press!*" he cried into the wind, ignoring the drums and the stares of dismay among the blacks when they saw he was not an angel of the Lord.

"What? ... What did you say?" I shouted back.

But he only took my picture and then began to pan the village with his 16mm. I knew the blacks were more afraid of him than they were of the roaring helicopter. He looked formidable with his bags of film and black boxes and yellow paper. I caught his arm and tugged at him. The pilot was loading cartons of medicine and my old CB radio. Behind him lay the rough-hewn altar, smashed by one inhuman wheel of the great *eropleni* as it came to rest in our place of worship. Nathan, the youngest boy, was trying to put the pieces together, his bronze face wet with tears. I was still holding the reporter's arm.

"What do you think you're doing here!" I yelled.

He started to speak but just then noticed the gaunt black child, sitting under the helicopter, holding the broken cross against his heaving chest.

"Wait! Wait a minute, that's priceless!" he cried.

"No! No!" I screamed as I jerked the camera from his hand, nearly collapsing beside him, and he seemed to really be aware of me for the first time. He leaned closer to me.

"Don't you understand," I said, struggling with the words. "He'll be dead within the hour!"

"Oh, Jesus," he swore, with sudden realization of the violence around us, grabbing my hand and pulling me toward the helicopter.

I resisted. I had to, but I knew that finally I would go with him. He gripped my arm so hard I had no time to think. The drums became part of the earth over which we stumbled. I saw the fiery sky, the wild green trees, the blood-brown path to Huzuni, the tortured eyes in the black faces. I must not go!

But I was going, and with this callous man from the *London Free Press*, who had come into the war-torn tribal land for a rich story, not for this resistant white girl seemingly bent on her own death.

"Nathan! … Nathan, come with me!" I caught his arm and implored with my eyes. There was a brief hope in that child's face, but the pilot shook his head.

"The white woman only!" he shouted. "Now!"

And I had to let him go, to watch the light drain from his being, the utter disbelief that I would not take him, and he ran.

The reporter half-carried me into the helicopter and slammed the door, and in seconds it seemed my people were tiny specks on the shattered ground—but not before I saw them thrashing their crosses and raising their fists to the sky, my message of the goodness of God a futile myth in those moments. I left them with a story they would never believe again.

"How long?" Stone was asking.

"About an hour," the pilot answered. "We're fighting this damned headwind."

We flew in silence over the death-dark woodland. The sun rose and revealed more devastation, burning huts and families crouched around their wounded and their dead. Jim Stone watched but did not take any pictures. He looked uncomfortable, maybe because of the choppy air or maybe because he had dragged me out of the compound so roughly. There was no way to talk, and so I reached over and put my hand on one of his still clutching a camera, a thing I had never done, touching a stranger like that. He kept his face turned toward the window, but in a few moments, he entwined his fingers in mine and did not let go until we landed in Dar es Salaam one hundred miles away.

When the horrendous noise of the engine and rotors had died, he looked at me.

"Maybe we should start over," he said.

"I think we already have," I answered with a quick smile.

Then he was gathering his equipment, and I my small bag of belongings, and it seemed an unlikely moment lost in the tumult of where we were and why we were there.

✢ ✢ ✢

I had some misgiving as we stepped out into the brisk forenoon in the busy seaport town. I had only been here once, when I first came to Africa. I was not prepared for the conflicting sounds or the people, black and brown and white faces jumbled together everywhere I looked. In the backcountry, I had almost forgotten that my own skin was white. And then the name Dar es Salaam held a sad and undeniable irony, for it meant "haven of peace." Ah, that dark transition from Huzuni to Salaam, from the misery of Christ to the place of peace without Christ. But I could not go back. *If Christ was ever in me, then He will be here, too,* I thought.

But still I did not move. I did not know where to go. Mr. Stone saw my hesitation and said, "Can I take you someplace?"

When I didn't answer, he said, "Will you stay with me for a while? I have a story to write. Remember?"

"My story?"

"If you'll tell me all of it."

"From the beginning?" I asked.

"I want to know everything," he answered. "Come on," he said quickly. "I know a little place …"

And before he had finished, he had waved down a rusty yellow taxi with a grim-faced driver who sped off along the narrow, crooked streets. We sat back in the cab, our shoulders almost touching, and I could think of nothing but the warmth of his hand in mine on that turbulent flight out of Huzuni, a white hand trying to ease my mind about what was happening to the only hands I had known for years, black hands. He was smiling, half-amused, half-serious, and I questioned him with my eyes.

"I was just thinking that I don't usually use that line on missionaries."

When I didn't react, he went on. "About the 'little place,'" I mean.

"Oh …"

"You have been out there a long time, girl!" he teased.

"Not long enough, I guess."

"Listen, Miss Pavane, I don't mean to make light of what happened in your village. I think it's only the beginning. I think we have to brace ourselves for a lot worse. Can you stand being in the city till things settle down?"

"If the Lord can use me here, I will be all right," I replied honestly.

"You are really sold on this Bible business, aren't you?"

"It's all I know, Mr. Stone," I said defensively.

"Journalism is all I know," he said, "but it seems to me much less confining, much less rigid."

"And much less rewarding," I reminded him.

"Maybe," he said. "It depends on what you want out of life."

"And what do you want?"

"I want you to call me Jim."

"Here's your stop," the driver was saying.

Almost the minute we sat down in the dimly lit restaurant, Jim said softly, "I'm sorry about the boy."

"Nathan … his name is Nathan."

"Well … it didn't seem right to leave him … and taking his picture, just a reflex. It seems that I live for the next great shot … not for life itself."

"Very profound, Mr. Stone … Jim. Maybe when you start living for life itself, your photos will get better."

"Is that a Christian teaching?" he asked, smiling again.

"No … but maybe it should be. After today, my Christian teachings don't seem to apply to life."

"I wouldn't go that far, dear girl," he said. "I'm sure you lived your Christian life very well."

"Until the end."

"The end?"

"When I lied to the faithful. I told them we would all be rescued."

"You didn't have much control over that, I'm afraid." He paused, and then asked, "What will you do now?"

"I have no idea. Huzuni was my home."

"Mine is even farther away," he said, "but I don't want to go back. I love this country. I want to tell its story, show the many faces, the people who are—how did you put it? 'Living for life itself.'"

"You may quote me, if you wish," I said.

"Hm, sarcasm in one so young. You'd make a good reporter."

"I am a missionary. I work for God."

"We'd better not talk about God."

"Why not?"

"Because I don't want to lose you so soon."

"Why would talking about God take me away from you?"

"Because I don't believe in Him," he said simply.

"All the more reason for me to stay and tell you about Him."

"No, thank you. All I want to know is why a beautiful, young woman like you would bury herself in the darkest part of Africa for four years of her life."

"If you want to hear that story, you are going to have to hear about God."

He shrugged and pulled out his frayed yellow notepad.

"You can't leave God out of this, Mr. Stone."

He would have spoken, but a white-aproned, grinning waiter now stood over us with his own small notepad. Suddenly I was very tired, and I let Jim order for me, not listening to what he said, not caring what I ate. I liked him in spite of his sharp edges, but I was afraid of him. Would he tear down with his pen what I had struggled to build in my forgotten corner of this land? Would he ridicule me because I loved God? Surely I could tell my story in such a way that he would soften, that he would at least acknowledge the purpose of my whole life.

"Miss Pavane?"

When I did not answer, he put his hand on my arm, and I shivered. His touch was sympathetic, and I had a new fear. I really didn't want to like him.

"Reena?"

I couldn't look at him.

"The thing is, Reena," he went on, "I am in the habit of pushing people, of getting a story at all costs, of printing the sensational side of human affairs. I don't know how to talk to a missionary."

"My story is not so sensational," I said more calmly now, though my body still trembled under his hand. "Where would you like me to start?"

"At the beginning," he said.

And I gave form, the form of words, to what had only been dreams and memories until now. I spoke swiftly, and he wrote furiously of things of the spirit, of God's will, of suffering and of joy, all with the same hurried scrawl, the same bemused expression. He never said an unkind word as the day wore on.

✝   ✝   ✝

I will always remember the moment my father came into the classroom. It was junior history, and I was bored, but I did not appreciate the sight of him striding vainly in, pushing a large white envelope under my teacher's questioning eyes.

"Reena, you may be excused," she said, and I went out into the hall behind my father's stiff back.

"The letter is here," he said, even before the door had closed. "Dr. Reiman is asking for us. It is time, my child. The Lord has called."

"Father, school is almost over ... then I can go."

"You will go now," he said sternly. And then more gently, as he steered me down the hall, "My daughter, do you not wish to serve the Lord?"

"Of course," I answered, wondering if I really meant it.

"We are leaving a week from today," he said. And he would not hear another word.

Thus I found myself stepping out onto African soil and calling it home before my sixteenth birthday. Oh I wanted to be a missionary. I had thought of little else for years. But I wanted to finish high school, to say good-bye to my friends, to my country, in my own way. As it was, it seemed like such a rash decision.

The first year, I was miserable, the name of the village to which we were assigned appropriate to my mood ... Huzuni ... misery. But I finally realized that my misery was so small compared to Christ's. I was humbled and vowed to put my heart into the work we had been commissioned by God to do.

After that, it was easier to teach the Word. What meaning did that

Dalton High diploma have when I could lead a hundred lives to salvation? I learned the African language, I survived in the mountains without all the conveniences of American life, and I shared the story of God with eager children and grandchildren of the hard-hearted, unreachable ones.

"But weren't you ever sick or afraid?" Jim Stone broke in.

"Yes … but that made me one of them, to suffer what they suffered."

And soon I was leading the blacks to the Lord on my own. My parents were busy organizing prayer meetings and clearing brush to build schools and churches. They stood over them, keeping themselves a bit apart, praying in English, and healing without touching them. I lived among them and prayed with my hands in theirs and sang in the language of their forefathers and was healed myself. We were one, the black and the white, and I vowed never to break that covenant.

"But I have broken it, you see. I have cut myself off from them and thrown up a wall between black and white. I left them."

"No, Reena," he said. "You had to. There was no reason for you to die. It wouldn't have made any difference!"

"You don't know that."

"Yes … I do. You were meant to come here. Maybe you don't see why yet, but I feel it, and I am the greatest doubter in the world. I feel the power in your life, in your being alive!"

"But it isn't my power, Jim. Without God, I am nothing," I said truthfully to this intense, unpredictable man from the *London Free Press*.

He leaned back in his chair, watching me. He had not written anything down for a long time.

"What is it?" I asked.

"I want to write your story, but I'm not at ease with the God part."

"Why? It's the reason I'm here."

"But converting people to your truth. It doesn't seem right."

"Look, I don't know if what I teach is literally true, but the lessons of love … that changes lives. It's not a conversion really. It's an opening to a Presence that's already there."

"An opening … now there's a scary thought. It seems to me that's a good way to get hurt."

"Not by God," I said quietly.

"What happened to your parents?"

"God sort of used them up, you could say. They went back to the States last year. They write now and then. I think they needed to feel safe."

He started to respond but then grabbed my hands with both of his and pressed them to his forehead.

"You're burning up!" I cried.

"Part of my story … malaria. Drugs help."

He reached into his pocket and took out a couple of pills. He seemed to breathe more easily after he'd taken them but said, "I need to get out of here. Will you be all right?"

"No … I have no place to go."

He hesitated and then led me out into the fading day.

"I have an apartment just down the street, extra bedroom … if you want it."

"I'm not leaving you, so I guess I have no choice."

"You just want to save my soul."

"Maybe I am more than a missionary, Mr. Stone," I said.

"That you are," he replied in a whisper.

We reached his rooms in a weathered, old hotel on a quiet hillside street. The contrast from the busy town was soothing in itself. The chloroquine seemed to be working, and so he let go of my arm. We sat on a small sofa that faced a large window with a view of the sprawling city and the distant sea. I felt safer than I had felt in a long time, but the situation was still awkward. We seemed to be at a loss for words.

"I hope you'll stay long enough to see my better side," he said finally.

"Oh, I think I've seen a bit of that," I said.

"The spare room is just down the hall on the right, if you want to rest. Later we'll go get you some decent clothes."

"I look like a street urchin," I said, glancing at my torn dress and dirty boots.

"You look like an angel," he replied.

"You're the only one who would say that now," I said, but I thought maybe I was crazy for imagining I could trust this stranger, this godless man. Still, I was curious. His place was neat and clean, with many books piled around for quick reference or enjoyment. He had a wonderful face, blue-gray eyes, and a gentle demeanor, in spite of the rough moments in Huzuni. He was probably ten or fifteen years older than I, and the weariness from his hours spent trying to "get the story" showed, his vulnerability to the malaria. I wanted to be there, with him, but I must not, must not let him see how I felt when he touched me. There would be no room for God in my heart.

We rested awhile in our separate rooms. I heard him moan in pain a couple of times but could not will my feet to go that way. I tried to pray, but the words seemed hollow and false. I had left my people and my God in that beautiful valley miles away.

When I got up, he was on the phone.

"Yes, Major Sommers, I understand … yes, I want the story. I'll put a few things together … in a week or so … okay." He hung up.

"Going someplace?" I asked.

"I'm not sure, don't really feel like it, but it's a good chance to see all this tribal conflict up close. Sommers called me first, knowing I was with the *London Free Press*. I'll be gone a couple of weeks. You'd have the place to yourself."

"I think I'd like those two weeks with you," I said, surprising us both.

"Reena, Reena, where is God when you need Him?" he said, laughing.

"Oh, He'll set me straight pretty soon, I'm sure!"

"Well, while you're waiting, let's go shopping and have some dinner."

✛   ✛   ✛

It felt like walking into a cave, that early evening air, healing and cool. We bought some clothes, Jim for his upcoming trip into the forest, and I some modern city clothes in shops owned by natives. We passed people dancing in the streets and a couple of flute players creating their haunting African melodies. It was easy to be with him. We found beauty in the same things: the sun going down through acacias and baobabs; a bright orange star bursting through storm clouds like a chunk of molten lava pouring through the branches of time; a mother buying her triplets ice cream, three different flavors; the sound of church bells singing out over all the human cadence like the voice of God. Well, Jim wouldn't go quite that far! But I was reminded of my true mission, hearing those bells and seeing those black faces all around me.

I was lost, however, almost drugged by the events of the morning. *Could this be the same day I abandoned Huzuni? Could I be the same missionary girl, wanting to slip my arm through Jim Stone's in the waterfalls of unreal light pouring down?* While I thought it, he took my arm and put it through his, and a lump came into my throat.

We ate dinner in a "little place he knew." It began to be a joke between us. We ordered African food, which was served by tall, handsome blacks all dressed alike, speaking graciously to their customers, in spite of perhaps the racists at some tables.

"I wonder if they're Christians," I said, referring to the blacks.

"Probably not, Reena. Does it matter?"

"I don't know. Why would I be so passionate about saving their tribal kinsmen and not them?"

"These guys might be harder to convince ... of anything, much less your God."

"But God is everybody's God," I said.

"Are you sure?"

Right then I wasn't sure of anything.

"Don't you believe in God at all?" I asked breathlessly.

"What I believe in doesn't matter. I've seen too much hate and ugliness and treachery. If I took you back to that village, to Huzuni, to the people you tried to teach about God, they'd cut your head off and not bother to bury you! God? What does He care about these blacks? They're out there killing each other off right now. For that matter, what does He care about you?"

"He sent you to me in that helicopter," I answered.

"Whoa ... great gift ... a middle-aged cynical guy with malaria. Thank you, God."

"I do thank Him."

A striking black man was standing over us.

"Would you care for dessert or wine?"

"Maybe in a little while," Jim said, and after the waiter left, "This conversation is like dessert and wine for me."

"Why?"

"Because it is something I can savor. Being with you is something I can savor, I can take with me into the backcountry."

And then I thought, oh what a victory over the slaughter in the hills, to lead this man to Christ. But somehow I never reached him with my message of salvation. I never told him that simple, sad, and glorious truth, because something happened. Something always happens when your own will gets in the way. I fell helplessly and unalterably in love with him.

Black

✧ ✦ ✧

I saw them pass by the first time and questioned their appearance, their easy familiarity, their even being together, and I said to myself, *Simple. Classy English journalist … whore.* And I went back to my work. I had heard rumors about the fighting in the hills, that there was nothing left of my ancestral village, that soon the militants would be inside the city itself, and I went on with my work. I felt secure; nothing could hurt me—I, Dakimu Reiman, with a Christian soul, an educated mind, an employed body. I did not have to get involved. I did not have to weep or wipe the eyes of my friends or the blood from their wounds. I was immune. And those two, that white reporter, that lowly *kahaba*, they especially could not touch me. I felt in that moment, barely glancing at their retreating shapes, the most arrogance I had ever felt in the twenty-three years of my existence.

But those two, those two that I so misjudged, brought to that existence the most meaning and the most pain that I thought possible for one man to bear. And I did not know it then, but I was about to embark upon the darkest journey of my life, a journey that would lead me blindly and desperately through hostile lands, across oceans I had not yet dreamed of, through a web of love and hate, tribulation and ecstasy.

And she and I will tell the story. We will inscribe it on your heart.

White

When we returned to the hotel, there was a sealed message for Jim from the British Embassy. It read with vague authority: *representative British Intelligence, will arrive 12 noon Thursday one week, Dar es Salaam Airport, regarding TS mission. Please meet.*

"Well, here it comes," he said with a sigh.

"What, Jim?"

"The special assignment I've been given. Only now … I don't really want it anymore."

"Because of me?" I asked.

"Partly … and then I'm not comfortable getting involved in the politics or with the military."

"But that's part of the story, isn't it?"

"I'm afraid it is … but now you're part of the story."

"I'll go with you."

"I don't think that will be allowed."

"But I speak the language. Natives know me."

"Not all natives, my dear."

"Then I have one week to find out who I am," I said, not thinking he would really understand what I meant.

"Reena … I can't let you stay with me."

"Why not?"

"Oh God, you are so innocent."

"Maybe I already lost my innocence. I have betrayed my friends, I have forgotten how to pray, I want to be with a stranger—"

"Am I such a stranger?"

"Yes, a stranger still, even though something in me wants you not to be."

"My dear little missionary, I am a married man, older but not necessarily wiser. I do not want you to forget your God."

"Maybe instead *you* will find *Him*."

"I doubt that. It's not on my agenda."

"Don't you need some time to hear the rest of my story?"

"That I do," he said softly.

Instead, I got him to tell me his story.

He had lived his first year in Africa in a village much like Huzuni, and it was there he had contracted malaria. In spite of his illness, he had wanted to remain in the land. He had made many friends among the blacks. He had challenged his readers all over the world to open their minds and their hearts to different ways of life. He had grown to love the rich, brown plains, the tangled, verdant hills, the crystal streams, and the power of the rivers at flood tide. He had felt at home in a straw-thatched hut and beneath a billion stars. He had dreamed of writing of the beauty and the vastness and the terror and the loneliness of this wild African land.

He spoke some about his wife, Nadine, who was talented and beautiful but not happy with his need to travel far and wide for a story. He didn't blame her.

"She came here once about a year ago," he said. "It didn't go well. I should have known this country wouldn't suit her. You don't need to know the details."

He seemed not to be able to go on. The sounds of the city had diminished. We sipped slowly the wine Jim had brought home from dinner and didn't need conversation, each lost in the separate realities that had thrown us together. When we finally said good-night in the hallway, Jim took my hand and pressed the palm to his heart. And it was enough.

In the morning, it was raining. Jim worked on his story, saying he may need to return to my experience in the history of Huzuni and the people there. I read some of his articles from the stacks of magazines. They held great empathy for the natives, their sometimes simple, sometimes complex lives, for the struggles of blacks in their own land with the whites who would dominate and control them. There was nothing about missionaries.

The poetry of his language made me wonder how this man could not see God. One manuscript began:

The day's red dawn pervaded my senses, lashing my being with its power, lifting my heart far above the waking world, the strange, sometimes inhospitable land. And in spite of the heat and the pain and the loneliness of the African realm, I was glad to be alive …

At noon, Jim fixed us sandwiches and tea, and we listened to the rain now pouring down on Dar es Salaam with a kind of violence.

"The rivers will be rising," he said. "We're supposed to cross the Rufiji on this little adventure." He hesitated. "I'd tell you more, but that's about all I know. Something big, I'd guess. I don't think Major Sommers knows the extent of it."

I thought of the drums in their death beats, my Christian natives caught in the firestorm of tribe against tribe. How many would still believe in their Savior? I had opened their eyes to God, and God must open them again. There seemed to be no place for mercy in this tale.

"Do you feel like talking about Huzuni?" Jim asked.

"I just don't know what angle you're looking for."

"I thought I knew when I flew into the jungle to get you, but now I'm not so sure. Let's start with why you stayed after your parents left."

"I believed in my calling," I said.

"To bring blacks into your white vision, or maybe I should say your white *version* of the world."

"No. To show them a way to God through Jesus."

"How do you know they hadn't found a way?"

"They had never heard the Bible. They needed that chance of all chances to live a holy life."

"So what did you first say to them?"

"I told them how Jesus came to die for them, that their sins were forgiven by His sacrifice on the cross."

"And what sins were those?" Jim asked.

"That was the hardest to explain, because I wasn't quite sure myself. I just said everyone sinned because we were human. 'Even white people?' they asked in amazement. 'Especially white people,' I assured them. 'So in that, we are equal,' a village elder said. 'We are equal in all ways,' I told him."

"Girl, you were ahead of your time," Jim said.

"I don't think so. Jesus lived two thousand years ago. What do you think He would have said?"

"Good point." He nodded. "Then what did you do?"

"We baptized them in the river and called them Christian. Sometimes hundreds would show up for that. They loved rituals. We gave up on the Ten Commandments though. That didn't exactly translate into their culture. Then what I feared the most began to happen. They began to judge each other and tribes who were different, who didn't follow Huzuni's dogma. So I changed my message. I only read them the New Testament. You know, 'Judge not lest you be judged,' and 'Love thy neighbor … '"

"'Do unto others' … I get it."

"But the more Christian they became, the more they were feared and hated by their distant brothers. It wasn't safe for kids to wander out of sight of their parents or for girls to go to the river for water by themselves. We drew together as a community. They trusted my God to take care of them. That helicopter was supposed to be ten helicopters to rescue them from the tumult."

"Now my story could be to find ones who survived," Jim said, "to see through those eyes, maybe a different kind of truth."

"Well, I guess you'll get your chance. If that's where you're determined to go."

He closed his eyes, and a brief pain passed through his body.

And so, that night, unbidden I placed my hand against his heart and said, "God be with you, Jim Stone." And he didn't flinch away.

Black

I saw the reporter and the girl again, walking the streets. He stopped and bought her a single white rose. Fitting … white rose, white girl. She must not be a whore. But who is she? I couldn't take my eyes off of them. The reporter … I thought his name was Stone … had been around five or six years. He appeared to enjoy the ambiance of East Africa and wrote thoughtful and well-researched articles about all aspects of our life. But he was white. What could he really know?

"Dak! Quit daydreaming and wash those trucks!"

"Yes, sir, Major Sommers, sir!"

White

✧　◆　✧

The third day after being wrenched from Huzuni, we went to the mission hospital for more malaria drugs. The nurse didn't recognize me until I said my name.

"Reena ... Reena Pavane!" she exclaimed. "I thought you were in Huzuni."

"I was evacuated a few days ago."

"And the others?"

"I don't know. Most of them ran away."

"Well, they'll be lost now, I suppose," she said accusingly.

"I had no choice," I said, but it sounded false.

"What do you want?"

"My friend, Mr. Stone, needs some chloroquine. He'll be going ... out of town for a while."

"I'll get a doctor for you."

"Thanks."

Jim put his arm around me and said, "Reena, don't mind what she thinks. Remember the 'judge not' lesson?"

"That's the most difficult one for everybody, I guess."

Jim spoke to the doctor for a moment and got a prescription for the drugs. He shook Jim's hand and then walked over to me.

"I knew your folks, Pierre and Sondra. Fine people," he said. "I heard what was happening in Huzuni and wondered how you'd deal with it."

"It wasn't my finest hour," I said.

"I'm glad you're safe, anyway," he said and turned away.

We stepped out into a bitter wind. Clouds piled up over the African hills like huge avalanches ready to descend upon black and white, saved and unsaved. We took shelter in a small café and ate in silence. That night, when I touched his heart in the hallway, he clasped both his hands over mine and seemed to not want to let go.

"Such a healing, Reena ... such a healing."

"For me, too," I said, and we parted in the dark hall.

✛   ✛   ✛

The fourth day brought terrible news. The militant forces, the Vitani, had crushed three villages. The city relatives gathered in despairing groups to receive messages from the mountains. I tried to speak to some of the natives, but Jim pulled me away when the voices became angry. Jim didn't even take any photographs, afraid of the crowd's reaction.

Back at the hotel, Jim finished up a couple of assignments and went to his room. I sat on the sofa, facing the storm-colored day. I felt such peace being with Jim. I thought of all the reasons I shouldn't be there, touching him every night in the twilight hall, but craving that moment so much that it scared me. I tried to imagine what it was going to be like without him in the next room, being across from him at the meal table, him reaching for my hand. It seemed a black, unfathomable event like my exit from Huzuni.

We ate in that night as the rain pounded our tile roof and thunder careened off the mud-laden hills.

"Maybe you won't have to go," I ventured.

"Hah! The military prides itself on physical challenges. I just hope the jeep has a roof."

I knew the story meant everything to him—the secrecy, his part in revealing another piece of Africa. He asked me should he take this, should he take that, hoping to capture me in his drama. I could barely keep from crying.

That night, holding my hand against his heart, he said, "Now this is living for life itself."

And it comforted me.

✤ ✤ ✤

Day five, a fiercer storm swept over Dar es Salaam. There were messages from Major Sommers and phone calls in some kind of code. I found myself curling in upon the reality of Jim's leaving. To keep me distracted, he wrote a few more pages about Huzuni.

"How did you know when the blacks really believed?"

"When they learned to sing 'Jesus Loves Me' in English, when they put away their war spears and took Communion with tears on their faces. It was a lot of things. My parents always wanted them to speak in tongues, but that concept totally dismayed them. 'But, Reena, English is hard enough!' they would say."

"Do you speak in tongues?" he asked.

"Only Swahili," I replied.

"Who were the easiest to convert?"

"Oh, the children, of course. They loved the stories of the baby Jesus and how he treated friends and enemies with the same devotion. The adults liked the songs and the prayers. Were they Christians? They vanished into the night and turned up in pagan camps; they smashed their crosses and burned their churches. But the children always came back to me."

"Would you have died with them?"

"If I had died, I could no longer tell the Good News."

"If you had died, you could no longer tell it to me."

"You seem to be doing all right without my Christianity."

"Can you be separated from your Christianity?"

"I thought leaving my congregation might have done that. I feel changed since that day. I can't explain it."

"Have you ever been in love?" he asked suddenly.

"Only with Jesus," I replied quickly.

And then, that night, I took his hand and put it on my heart, and neither of us said a word.

✛   ✛   ✛

The morning of the sixth day broke bright and clear. Everything sparkled with new light—the whitecaps on the sea, the mirrors of cars on the crowded streets, the still-wet leaves of the city's trees.

My throat ached. It felt risky to speak. Again and again, the phone rang, and Jim's voice, too, became hoarse and strained. Finally we collapsed on the couch and just let the serenity of the view calm us. The Indian Ocean rippled with pearly waves and flashes of cobalt blue, a moving painting that soothed and stirred at the same time.

After a time, Jim said, "I'm going out to the base early in the morning, take all my bags and check in with Sommers, then I'll come back … to spend a couple of hours with you."

"I'll be very glad for that time."

"Think it'll be enough to save my soul?" he teased.

"Probably not," I said, "but I'll take whatever I can get."

"Do you think I need to be saved, Reena?" he asked more seriously.

I hesitated. "Only from me, Jim. Only from me."

He smiled such a generous smile, and then there was a long space with no words.

At dinner, we met John Sommers at a restaurant in a white neighborhood but spoke of nothing military. No one seemed worried. Business as usual, but I could barely eat.

Later, we spoke briefly of it.

"Did you like being in that room full of whites?" I asked Jim.

"No, not at all. Sommers told me our mission involved things some blacks would find offensive, and he didn't want any so-called black informers to head for the hills ahead of us."

"A British reporter having dinner with a British Major is suspicious?" I asked.

"Apparently so."

"I don't have a very good feeling about this," I said. "I will pray for your safety, if you don't mind."

"Reena, right now I wouldn't mind if you threw me in the river and baptized me!"

"Be serious," I said.

"I think it will take more than a river, my angel," he sighed.

✢   ✢   ✢

When we stood in the hallway that night, we looked at each other for a long time. I thought he was going to take my hands and hold them against his heart, but instead he leaned down and kissed me, so, so sweetly and just long enough.

"One for the road, Reena Pavane," he said.

"One for the road, Jim Stone."

Black

✧　◆　✧

I thought it a strange request, at dawn, when I was summoned by Rand Healy of the British Embassy, Intelligence Division. The voice had been hushed and secretive as it gave me the orders: have a jeep ready at 0700, top condition, full tanks, two extra gas cans, twenty gallons of water, military-band shortwave radio, two survival kits, two sleeping bags, rations for sixty days, forty-five long-range signal flares. I wrote down each item with growing wonder, but I did no questioning. I did my job. No names were included in this list, no driver, no passenger. It was odd, but then so were the times, and I was only a black.

As I worked on the jeep, I tried to more clearly define my apprehension. There had been trouble between the British Air and Ground Patrol and the militant blacks, the Vitani forces, who had been plundering peaceful villages for many months and defying the semblance of law and order established by the British for the protection of visitors, foreigners with capital interests in the land, and hard-working, cooperative natives alike. The Vitani called these efforts interference, and they had begun a campaign of terror that was sure to cause retaliation, not retreat. I knew that soon, perhaps today, a high-echelon leader in the British Intelligence, Colonel Edmunde Hahlos, was to be met by a reporter from the *London Free Press* who had been residing in this country for a considerable number of years. I thought fleetingly of the lean, sun-browned man I had seen a few days ago with the *kahaba* in the street. He was probably the one. Now he would have to leave his new pleasure for his new assignment. Hah! What did I care. I had my job.

At 0900, the jeep stood clean and ready, all equipment checked and double-checked, all mechanical parts tested carefully. No one could ever say Dakimu Reiman caused this mission to fail, whatever it was. I had followed my orders to the letter, although I still felt uneasy. And I experienced even more anxiety when, at 0945, Major Sommers appeared. As my immediate superior, he had developed a smooth relationship with me, and his directives were never given in a condescending way. He showed genuine liking for me and indifference to the color of my skin. This man now said, pretending to scrutinize the vehicle assigned to me, but watching for my reaction, "Is she set to go, Dak?"

"Yes, sir … a bit early, if I may say," I answered.

"You may not say."

I had heard others in the unit talking about Hahlos. "I understood the Intelligence man would not arrive until noon, and then would not leave for another hour," I said, trying to learn more.

"There has been a change. He put down an hour ago and does not wish to wait. The river is rising, recent storms and more bad weather up-country. And the reporter will be here soon. He should be willing to go ahead of schedule."

"I suppose so, sir."

"By the way, Dak, after they're gone, you are to tell no one of this departure. I'm sorry I can't explain more. I really don't understand the entire set-up myself."

And I believed that day that he really meant it, although the events to come would devastate any trust that I had placed in the words of white men. I promised to keep quiet about the unusual behavior of the participants in his little drama, but I was not through probing with my mind and my eyes into every act, every scene that developed. I was only a black to them, but they should not have discounted my curiosity and my perseverance.

The play began to unfold swiftly then. The reporter came in, hurried and rather pale, I thought. He glanced at me and turned to Major Sommers.

"John, what's going on? We're not leaving!"

The major ignored his question and said, "Mr. Stone, this is Dakimu Reiman. He has prepared the jeep carefully for your expedition. I hope everything is satisfactory. Now, if you will excuse me." He began walking away nervously. "Good luck, Jim," he added, still moving back from the bewildered newsman, the same who had laughed into the eyes of the *kahaba*.

Jim Stone grabbed my arm, not unkindly, and said sharply, "We're not supposed to go for hours. Why now?"

"Those are your orders, not mine," I said briskly. His discomfort was no concern of mine.

"I'm sorry, young man," he said apologetically. "It's not your fault. But do you know why?"

"No, sir."

"But there is someplace I have to go first."

I thought of the long-haired, beautiful girl and turned away as Major Sommers had from his anxious face.

"You'd better ask *him*," I said.

He swung around. Striding toward us importantly was Colonel Edmunde Hahlos. He nodded to me, as if in dismissal, and grasped the reporter's outstretched hand vigorously.

"Jim Stone! You old dog! So it's you! I'm glad. We understand each other! Is this our transportation? Looks fit for a king. Hah! Let's hope the *mfalmes* don't steal it!"

He said all of this in one confident breath. Mr. Stone looked even more surprised. He tore his hand from the colonel's and spoke adamantly.

"Edmunde, regardless of our long association [I noticed he didn't say friendship] and understanding, I'd like to know what is going on! I was told to pick up a representative of your service at noon at the airport and that we wouldn't leave until one o'clock, that the mission would be outlined for me at that time. And what about your man coming in later?"

"My man?"

"The Intelligence agent."

"That's me, old boy! Your message was a decoy. Hopefully it was read by the right people, or should I say wrong people! By the time they have surrounded the airport looking for information or a way to delay me, we will be long gone. We're heading upriver, together, now! In fact, we are later than I planned. These your things here?"

"Yes, but …"

"Well, put them in, boy," the colonel said to me, acknowledging me when I was needed.

I hesitated, and the reporter reached for his bags.

"I believe I'm capable of that, Ed," he said with a strained half-smile that reprimanded the colonel for his discourtesy toward me and showed his own respect for me.

I began to load his things quickly.

"I'll be happy to do it, sir," I said, liking him immensely.

He was appealing to the colonel for time to do his errand. I was sure it had something to do with the girl, and I felt disappointed. Why did he hook up with such a woman? But I could be wrong about him, and her, too, I thought for the second time.

"Jim! Jim! There's no time now! I'm sorry. Our mission must begin now or it is lost." The colonel's voice rose above the wind and the clatter of machines in the yard. He forcefully shouldered Mr. Stone into the jeep and drove off without a backward glance.

I was extremely disturbed. In the first place, the reporter had seemed almost ill to me. And the colonel was in too much of a hurry. He did not check out with Major Sommers, who was still sitting in his office, a confused expression on his face, which he visibly tried to control when I walked in unannounced.

"I don't like it, sir," I said at once.

"You're not paid to like it, son."

"I spoke out of my concern for the newsman. I don't believe he was prepared for this sudden departure."

"But that's not your business, Dak," he reminded me. "It's out of our hands now. Go back to work and forget it."

"I will go back to work, sir, but I shall not forget it. There was too much pain in that man's face."

"Which man?"

"Jim Stone, sir."

"He accepted this assignment willingly enough," Sommers said.

"But I tell you he was not ready!"

"The affair is over, Dak. I don't want to speak of it again. Is that understood?"

"Yes, sir," I said and returned to work.

But I was still troubled. I tried to put the incident out of my mind, but the longer I worked in silence, the more I wanted to talk to someone about what had happened. I would hardly have believed then that the first person I would speak to would be the cheap *kahaba* from the streets of Dar es Salaam.

It could not have been a half hour before the girl came rushing into the yard. She looked different somehow, sweet and clean, but I turned my back on her.

"Please … could you help me?"

Her voice was soft, but I was still suspicious.

"What is it? I'm busy," I said without facing her.

"I … I'm sorry." She paused. "My name is Reena Pavane."

I was shocked. I had heard that name before.

"The missionaries' daughter?" I asked, amazed. "From Huzuni?"

"Yes."

"What are you … why … are you here?"

"The village … had to be evacuated," she said reluctantly. "Last week."

She seemed so frightened. I moved toward her and spoke softly. "Do not be afraid. I am a Christian … and honored to meet the teacher of my brothers." I bowed slightly, but she looked at me sorrowfully, and I knew what she was thinking: *Does he mean his blood brothers? Does he not know they are dead?*

I gazed back unflinchingly and said, "Huzuni was the home of my adopted family. I, myself, was raised there, but I came to the city to acquire more education and to work. I have been happy here, and I do not wish to talk of those events that you still fear."

"But will you talk of Jim Stone?" she asked hopefully.

"Yes ... he has gone," I began. Then I remembered. I was to tell nothing. Major Sommers had come out and was signaling to me frantically. I leaned closer to her and warned her, "It is top secret."

"I know! He told me as much as he knew, which wasn't a lot. But he was to meet me before he left. I have something for him ... something he must have."

"There is no way to catch him. What is it he needs?"

"Medicine ... for malaria."

"Ah ... I thought so. He did not look well."

"I must find him."

"The authorities would not grant permission."

"Would they permit him to die?" she said with anger.

"Is it so serious?"

"It could be, without the drugs."

"How do you know so much about this man?"

"He ... was with those who came on the helicopter ... to rescue me. We ... stayed together ... so he could write the story."

"Wait a minute. Helicopter? Only one?"

"Yes ... forgive me. It is so hard to tell you, since you must have known some of those that I left behind. You should not only refuse to help me, you should hate me, too."

"I should probably do more than that, if I were not a Christian."

"Your brothers forgot even that. When I rose alone into the sky, they smashed their crosses to the ground."

"Then that is your punishment. Do not condemn yourself more," I said gently to this compelling white missionary.

"What is your name?" she asked.

"Dakimu. I was baptized with the second name of Reiman, after my own teachers in Huzuni. I am called Dak."

"The Reimans brought us over four years ago," she said. "You were already gone. But now, Dak, will you help me?"

I decided to find out just how much she knew. "Who was with him?" I asked.

"A man from the British Intelligence on a diplomatic assignment, apparently wanting a good reporter to cover the story."

She knew too much already, and I whispered, "Listen, Miss Pavane, I cannot tell you more. I will lose my job. It is important to me."

"As important as a man's life?"

"Right now, yes!"

"Dak, I know they were going to cross the Rufiji River. Just tell me from there which trail might they take. I'll find him."

"You would risk your own life?"

"I would give my life," she said.

"Ah … I see it now. You care deeply about this man. I fear he is in grave danger, even if the malaria does not weaken him."

"Danger? Why? What is it?"

"I don't know. They tell me nothing, sometimes treat me like nothing. I should help you just to spite them."

"Who?"

"The British military and those who keep secrets about my country."

"Has Jim Stone kept secrets?"

"No … he has always told the truth in the things he has written and with compassion. I liked him today, when I met him for the first time."

"Then help me … to help him."

"I do not know where they have gone, but maybe together we shall figure it out."

The major was coming toward us, looking furious, shouting long before he reached us, "Dak! Send the girl to me! You have work to do."

"Say nothing, Miss Pavane—only that you came for a jeep and a driver to take you about the city in search of Huzuni's estranged families. Then wait for me. I'll be finished in a couple of hours. Can you wait that long?"

"Of course … I'll wait, but I don't know why you're doing this," she said.

"Neither do I, but go! He will be upon us!" I answered curtly.

"If you will come to the office, ma'am, perhaps I can help you," he broke in, out of breath and sweating in the midday sun. But he calmed a bit when he saw her.

"Why, Miss Pavane, I didn't know it was you! Could you have come from Huzuni only a week ago?"

"I did, Major."

"The helicopter found you all right?"

"Yes …"

"And now perhaps you wish our help in finding relatives of the people you had to leave?"

"Mr. Reiman has volunteered to drive a jeep for me, when he has finished his work … if you do not object."

"No, no, he may take you. He may know where some of these people are. His own people were from Huzuni, I believe …"

That is the last I heard. I watched them moving away, and then I worked quickly, partly to remove my mind from what had happened, and partly to end my present task and embrace the new one, the one still dark and unknown, the one that would not come to light until I committed myself to the heart of Reena Pavane.

She and I waited for such different things. Her mind was on saving a man she barely knew, and mine on discovering what kind of emotion it was that drove her to it. Did I have that in me? I read the Bible, I prayed the right prayers, I loved my enemies, but would I plunge out into the unknown, into forbidding and dangerous territory after a brief encounter with someone like that? Yes, he was suffering. Yes, she was a healer, but this was crazy. My heart beat faster at the thought of being with such a woman on such a journey, so far from my comfort zone, my principled life. Black and white in the maze of the African landscape like albatross at sea who do not find a place to land for years.

✝   ✝   ✝

She looked up at me from her post on the hard bench by the major's office.

"Is it time?" she asked.

"Yes … but are you sure you must do this?"

"I'm sure."

And that was the true beginning.

✢   ✢   ✢

The road twisted ahead of us through the wide green hills. Birds still sang in the early twilight, and the beasts of the field had come out to feed in close, restless bunches on the short grass. It was deceptively peaceful, the calm before the storm. Two storms, I thought—the one from the sky and the one from our hearts. Behind us lay the security of the city and the road ... a way back.

We pushed on into the black mask of night, unaware that tomorrow, had we desired, we could not have returned by the same path. Even God began to seem like an idea, not a reachable source of safety or resolve. We relied more and more on our own strengths, our own purpose. We aimed ourselves at the deadliest ground, at the crumbling bank of a flooding river, at the trembling drums of another world, at a place where no one spoke the name of God. I cannot answer for her, but as for myself ... I never found God again.

✢   ✢   ✢

We did not speak in the rocking, dusty cab, lost in our imaginations and not quite sure of each other yet. I don't think she was ever afraid of me. I became her last hope of reaching Jim Stone, and perhaps that is why she began to lean on me instead of our Savior. Sweet Jesus, you could not know her heart in this!

When I could not avoid the massive holes or the roots of trees that traversed the road like great wooden snakes, she clutched the bag that held the drugs tightly, and I slowed down.

"No! Please! We must cross the river tonight!"

But just as she cried out, the rain began to fall in torrents, nearly blinding me, until I got the wipers going, and if I had any doubts before, they were now confirmed. We would not ever cross the river. But she seemed undaunted by this possibility.

"They will have to stop in this storm! We can catch up a little," she said confidently.

"Yes," I said.

But the dread in my gut would not go away. My eyes remained fixed to the muddy track, and my hands to the jerking wheel. Suddenly we came upon the river. It swirled and crashed with a violence I had not known it possessed, and because the light was failing fast, we could not see the breadth of the crossing or the place on the opposite bank where we would emerge. We knew then from its terrible sound that it could not be traversed.

"We are too late," I said, somehow relieved. "I am sorry for Mr. Stone. He was kind to me. But I'm not sorry for us. There's more to following him than you know."

"Yes, yes, it's top secret!" she said with frustration. "If it's so secret, why on earth would they take a journalist? Why does our knowing it matter so much?"

"It matters to people you do not know."

"Where are they? Back in their comfortable chairs on their screened-in porches with their gin-and-tonics in hand?"

"Probably ... but you cannot change things."

"I can and I will! I'm not going back. I'll swim if I have to!"

I put my head in my hands for a moment and fought the idea that had begun to form. How could I want to do more for them? How could I even consider going on? But finally I said, "The storm will abate towards morning, and we can try to cross then. We will have to wait. Come."

I put the gears in reverse and backed up to higher ground. I made a shelter by stretching a canvas from one side of the vehicle to an overhanging boulder, securing it with large rocks and ropes to nearby trees. Besides being safe and dry, we were hidden from view. It would not be long before British troops were following us as we were following Jim Stone. Had he been taken against his will? Would they continue in this treacherous weather, with increasingly hostile natives in their path and the malaria wearing Jim down to the bone? It must be some secret indeed.

We sat in silence for a while, but she held me with her eyes. Did she see my body that was lean and hard, my manner that was soft and refined, my color that was unblemished, my youth corresponding with hers or anything beyond the fact that I was taking her to Jim Stone? She was huddled in one corner of our lean-to, her legs drawn up, her chin resting on her knees, her silky gold hair framing her suntanned face. Her beauty was ageless. I could not imagine lines on that brow or creases beside that mouth. Her beauty was spiritual, although when I said Jim Stone's name, a spark of animal fire flashed in her blue-green eyes.

Then she hid her face from me by putting her head on her knees, and the magnificent passion of those eyes was lost to me. I lit the lantern, which could be extinguished quickly, if need be, but did not build a fire, so we ate cold ham and peas from a can. She ate very little, and I forced myself to eat for what energy it might give me later on. I had brought a jeep as well-provisioned as the one taken by the colonel, on the pretense that the people Miss Pavane hoped to find might need aid of some kind. And it had worked. Major Sommers had smiled benevolently and wished us Godspeed. But it was past time for us to be back, and I imagined him not smiling so benignly. I could see him pacing around his cluttered desk, a grim expression on his face, a nervous twitching in his hands.

"Where are they?" he would mutter to himself. "A black man and a white girl alone, in this country, after dark. Goddammit!"

I had to laugh then, but Reena did not notice. I did not care for white women. I remembered the disgust I had felt when Jim Stone had walked by with Reena. But I had been wrong about her. So maybe I was wrong about myself. Why should I not like her or even love her, if I wanted. The color of our skin should not matter. I would not let it matter.

When she looked up at last, she said, "Dak? You are so good to do this for me ... and for Jim."

"It's not over yet."

"But I am in your debt. No matter what happens," she said softly.

We tried to sleep, but the river raged through our dreams. It was a tight space, so it was inevitable that we would touch in the night. I grieved that I had never made a friend like this or even wanted to know a white woman in any kind of significant way. Sitting next to Reena did something strange to my heart, and I wished that I could tell her.

In the morning, I rose and went down to the river and washed my face in the swirling water. It was still rising. I turned away from it, discouraged and not refreshed. I knelt down with my back to the monster for what seemed a long, long time. When I heard Reena's voice and opened my eyes, I was startled to see that she was ready to go.

"Dak? Are you all right?"

"I was praying," I lied.

"Turn around then," she said.

I did and could not believe what I saw. The water was a good ten feet from where I had stooped to wash my face! And it was not moving as swiftly or as threateningly.

"Let's go!" I shouted, racing up the hill to our camp. She had everything in the jeep, lashed down and covered.

"Can we make it now?"

"Maybe ... barely," I said.

I swung into the jeep, shifted into compound second as the engine engaged, and moved toward the torrent. I almost stopped before we hit the river, but I looked at the sky. It stared back senseless and defiant, and it filled me with that same wild emotion.

It has to be now! I cried to myself.

The wheels spun in the first, soft earth. I let up on the accelerator, and they took hold again, uncertainly. But we were off the bank, and there was no turning back. I had not counted on the damage to the roadbed beneath us—the heavily traveled ruts that I believed were still there, although I could see nothing through the ocherous mass. And the river was deeper, much deeper than it had ever been, for though the water had receded from the shore, it had done so only because now there existed deeper channels in the middle through which it could run! And the river was stronger than it had appeared from the bank. We began to rock and turn, and I struggled to keep the front end of the jeep headed upriver. I glanced at Reena. Her face was paling.

"We can't go back!" I yelled.

But either she didn't hear me or she was too stunned to answer, for she clung to the side of the jeep and stared straight ahead. We were less than halfway across. The jeep was filling with water, and we were barely moving forward. We had been flung about so that we were bruised and shaken, and finally we began to drift downstream, picking up speed with the rushing current, which was completely controlling us now—our course, our lives.

"Get out, Reena! Swim back! We still have a chance! Get out!"

Then she gave me a desperate look and dove over the open side, the side parallel to the shore we had left. But she let the jeep pass her, as it floated powerlessly, and struck out behind it for the opposite bank! I jumped out on that side, but she was already by me, and I could not reach her.

"Reena!" I screamed. "No!"

She fought on, away from me, slowly, relentlessly, and I could hardly keep my head above the roiling water. My feet plunged in mud and tangled vines close to a piece of the shore that jutted out into the river from the side that led to Dar es Salaam. All at once, I was free, free to go back and live, but I did not hesitate. I followed her.

It was easier in the current. I didn't have to fight it. I could let it carry me a few feet, and then swim, and then relax, and then swim. That's what she was doing a few yards away. But I noticed she kept glancing upstream, changing her direction as if dodging something, but I dared not let her out of my sight.

When the log hit me, I was totally unprepared. I went down for a moment, legs thrown upward by the force of the blow. I reached the surface in what seemed like hours, gasping for air and stroking again, but I could no longer swim! I was welded somehow to the big, forked branch and was hurtling with it downstream. I could not see what held me there, but I was part of it, and it would not let go. For an agonizing moment, I saw Reena even further downstream. She must have reached the center where the flow was faster. The log and I would soon be even with her, and then beyond her, and then lost to her sight.

"Reena!" I cried.

She turned. The current whipped against her, propelling her deeper into its grasp. She disappeared again and again, but I realized one thing. She was coming back! Or maybe letting herself be carried to a point where she would crash into me! She could have made it without me. She actually threw herself into the heart of the river, past a place where she could have pulled herself to safety. But here she was, beside me at last, nearly exhausted, grabbing my knife that was still clipped to my belt, slashing at my pant leg, at the vines wound around it, at the limb caught in blood-stained khaki. And then I was rolling without the log, back into the charging waves, through them, under them, into calmer eddies by the mud-caked shore, onto firmer ground with heaving sides and a pounding head, collapsing with Reena on the storm-eroded bank of the Rufiji.

We could not speak ... but suddenly, she sat straight up and let out a cry, staring down at the cruel river from whence we had come. "Dak! The serum! My God, the serum!"

I closed my eyes. I, too, had forgotten it in our frantic battle with the river. And then I was choking and gagging on the green-brown water I had swallowed. But Reena quickly slung her arm around my chest and held me until the worst had passed. I swear, in that moment, I loved her with my whole being. I had never needed an anchor, and here she was wrapping me in her own cut and bleeding arms.

I did not wish for her to ever let go. She caressed my back and whispered the Lord's Prayer into my ear. In her voice, it sounded true, and I let it fill me with peace. The prayer was still on her lips when I stopped her.

"Reena ... Reena. It hurts me to hear those words. I can't trust them anymore. I can't trust anything."

"We are together, and we are alive," she said. "Trust that."

"But we have nothing—no drugs for Jim, no weapons or food, no dry clothes."

"We have each other ... and God, our Father."

"No ... it is all mixed up in my mind with the death grip of the river and the foolishness of leaving my comfortable, sane life. The God from my city church, the God from my Bible study, the God from my Lenten fasting. That God is not here!"

"Maybe you are just seeing a different face of God."

"I see your face," I said, turning over, but she let go of me, and the communion was lost.

White

I bound his wounds with my torn clothing, I wept over the lost serum, and I didn't know whether to thank God or the river that we were alive. Dakimu hugged the earth as if it were his only friend.

"Let's get away from here," I begged him. "The water could rise."

Slowly he moved with me up to the road. I put my arm around him, and after we found a place to rest, I looked into his dark eyes.

"We are utterly in God's hands now," I said.

He shivered and cried into the oblivious gray skies, "This is not what God had planned for me! I cannot have been carried to shore by a white woman. I cannot owe anything to a white woman!"

He pounded the ground with his fists.

"Consider the debt canceled," I said gently. "And besides, it has to stop mattering that our skin is a different color."

"But you can't think that we can go on! I am trusted! I am respected in the city. Out here, I am worthless."

"Not to me, Dak. Not ever to me."

But he fell back and would say no more.

Black

When I awoke, Reena had gathered enough berries and roots to sustain us until morning, and she had found a clear spring from which she brought me fresh water in a rough bark cup she had fashioned with my knife. For two days, we stayed in that place, within the sound of the furious river that had tried to crush us. We hid within sight of the muddy ford that we had crossed but that our pursuers glared at in great frustration. We watched them pacing up and down, pointing to the narrow spots in the channel and arguing over what had happened and what to do.

I said to her once, "You could go out, and they would help you across, and you would be safe."

"What about you?" she asked.

I didn't answer right away. It seemed that the longer I stayed on the dark, unknowable side of the Rufiji, the more it satisfied me. I did not have to walk that thin line drawn for a black man in Dar es Salaam. I could be as wide and raging as the river behind us. I could be as godless and unpredictable as the surge of storm-water holed up in the hills, waiting to strike again. This new Dakimu appealed to me, and so I said, "I cannot go back now."

"I can't go back either," she said.

After a while, the men went away, but I knew they'd return, and so that night we took the most deeply worn footpath toward the forest and left the broad, safe road. We must have been a strange sight to the eyes of those first friendly natives we met on our journey. Many of them were refugees from camps and villages higher up where the aggressors were active, and I know Reena feared coming face to face with a black from Huzuni.

I told villagers she was my wife. Some city blacks had married white women, so it was not questioned. We said we were searching for two white friends in a jeep, who must be reached before they entered the territory of the Vitani. The peaceful blacks, the Tulivu, were very willing to help, even though the men we sought were white. Living closer to British stations, they were familiar with jeeps and hurried white faces, tourists and soldiers, and they sympathized with anyone who might be threatened by the militants.

"We have seen them down on the road. Stay on this trail and you will parallel their course," the elders told us eagerly.

It was inevitable, however, that as we plunged deeper into the wooded hills, we learned less and less from the native people. They became more suspicious and more reticent, and Reena and I became more wary. At first, we used the visits in the villages to take advantage of the blacks' kind offer of food, hiding what we could in the baskets and bedrolls that had been supplied by the natives who trusted us. Soon I was forced to leave Reena a short distance from the villages and beg for food and gain information in an indirect manner. And then, I had to hide her as much as two or three miles out, when we began to meet Vitani runners at their outposts.

Those were terrible times. I never knew if Reena would be there when I returned, if she would be raped or cut to pieces. I was plagued by dreams of desire and death, and none of it was real. I looked at the white woman who was traveling beside me, trying to be brave, and sometimes I wanted to fade into the bush, just be gone from her side, her life. But it was because of her that we were alive and that we were closer to saving the life of Jim Stone.

We learned that Jim and Colonel Hahlos were four days ahead of us, that they had some kind of information or goods they were trading for safe passage. Reena brightened a little, and I felt glad for her. We rested more often now. Our feet were badly blistered, our shoes long worn through and discarded. Our backs tired easily, and our arms ached from breaking through tamarind branches and knotted vines. Sweat poured from our bodies, and the summer sun boiled it on our flesh. Then the rains would come and revive us again.

We trusted each other in the beginning. We shared secrets and doubts about the meaning of our lives, even doubts about God. Being Christian was not the only thing common to us, and being black and white not the only difference. But I thought a lot about the white Jim Stone down the trail and Reena's quest to be with him. She had never said she loved him. What hold did he have on her? She had been with me now longer that she had with him. She had saved my life. We had outwitted blacks and whites alike, crawling through dark tunnels of trees and brush, raw as newborn calves with scrapes and burns. We had swum together in clear pools untouched by the massive runoff in the flood channels. I was the murky river; she the crystal pool. We had eaten off the land, when the friendly villages became fewer and farther between. I was the dark berries, she the golden maize. But we fit somehow. We struggled and cried and felt defeated, black and white bound like a poem in metaphors of reconciliation and hope.

But between us always was the countenance of Jim Stone.

One time, I tried to kiss her. I would never have hurt her, but she lunged away, afraid.

"Please, Dak, that can't happen."

"Because I am black?"

"No! Never that, Dak. You are a beautiful man. And you are my friend. I want you as my friend," she said adamantly.

But it was too late for me. I wanted so much more. I didn't call it love then, because I had so hated the idea of a white woman. But I would soon wish, more than anything, to trade places with Jim Stone.

White

Late one evening, Dak caught an African hare in a crude net he had made. It was the first meat we had had since the early friendly villages. We built a small fire and roasted the flesh slowly. A half-dozen hyenas circled hopefully, barking their expressive and melodious yips. We tossed them bones as we devoured the rabbit.

I studied Dak's face in the flickering firelight. He was heart-breakingly beautiful. His features were chiseled like an Ethiopian's, but his skin was dark. Even sitting on the rough ground, he looked tall and elegant, like a prince. He said he didn't know who his parents were, that he came from an orphanage near Kilimanjaro and was sent to Huzuni for the missionaries to tame his wild streak. The Reimans had tamed his temperament, baptized him, and given him their name. There was still a lost hue to his eyes, a direct gaze that was unsettling.

He was lean. I guess we both were at that time, subsisting on berries and corn left in some farmer's field and an occasional mango. We were as raw as the land, as hungry as the leopards we came across couched in a tree. They didn't bother us, but we gave them a wide berth. We had to abandon the trail a few times for elephants foraging for deeper grass. One day resting, we marveled at giraffes nibbling the tops of acacia trees and loping off at some perceived threat, although even lions rarely attacked those leggy beasts. It was a surreal and breathtaking world, but we were on a mission out of the animals' realm, and we mostly avoided their company.

Dakimu jumped up later that night at an unfamiliar noise. He pulled me into a thicket of strangler figs and held me tight. Out by our campfire a jackal nosed around in the smell of rabbit, and then, scenting us, scurried off. He released me quickly, and I said, "Dak, I'm not afraid of you."

"You should be," he said.

In the morning we moved on, not speaking, but not shying away when our shoulders touched or our hands met parting branches. It seemed that words would only ruin the shaky beginning of trust.

Black

It was that afternoon that we met Colonel Hahlos crossing a narrow northern valley in the Uluguru Mountains. I was moving cautiously, a few feet ahead of Reena, when I turned suddenly and motioned toward the tangle of undergrowth beside us. She disappeared silently, as we both had learned to do in this more hostile territory, and left me standing alone in the roadway. We had become so exhausted on the overgrown trail that we now stuck to the main track.

Hahlos was surrounded by ten huge blacks, and they closed in around him like thick, iron gates, holding up their rifles and shouting at me, "*Nenda! Nenda!* Go!"

I called back, our only chance, "Colonel Hahlos! Colonel Hahlos!"

The whole group halted some distance away, and a frightened voice came out of the human prison, "Who are you? What do you want?"

"Do you remember me, Colonel?" I asked.

He squinted against the sun. "Come closer," he said.

The guards stiffened, but I showed them I had no weapon in my hands, and they opened a small space in their garrison, revealing a thin, terrified old man. The jungle had wrought a change here. The once proud and confident colonel now seemed beaten and helpless. He shaded his eyes, which I could see were sunken and bloodshot, before he spoke.

"You ... from the British Air and Ground Patrol base ... in Dar es Salaam?"

"Yes ... I am Dakimu."

"Oh, my God!" he cried, recognizing me at last. "What are you doing out here? Did Sommers send you after us? Why would he do that? What does it mean? You can't take me from these people!" he babbled.

"I don't want you, Colonel," I said with some sarcasm.

He looked perplexed at that and said, "What then?"

"Jim Stone."

"You're too late!" he said almost immediately.

I heard Reena gasp behind me, but she remained hidden, and Hahlos went on, unaware of her presence. The blacks glanced about but could not place the sound and were finally satisfied that it could not challenge them.

"Colonel!" I wanted to shake some sense into him. "Is Mr. Stone dead, then?"

"No ... I mean, I don't know. By now I think he must be. He's got the malaria and was very weak. That's why they kept him instead of me," he explained, "part of the deal ... but you don't know anything about that," he added quickly.

"I intend to find out, Colonel."

"Then you are a fool! Come along with me. It's your only chance, boy!"

"I'll take my chances without you," I said with a smirk. "It is my country, Colonel."

"Yes ... of course," he said, beginning to look disinterested. "It's two days' journey from here, back along this trail. But you will not be welcomed, I can tell you that."

"It doesn't matter. I must go," I told him, beginning to walk past him.

"Another mission? Hah! We are all fools!" And he went off in his little prison, muttering and shaking his head deliriously.

The moment they were out of sight, Reena emerged from her secret place with a stricken face.

"Oh, Dak, he is lost to me forever!"

"I don't think so, Reena ... let's just go on."

And I took her hand and pulled her up the hill to the old trail. It would be safer there. She did not resist, though tired and disheartened, and I wondered at my own choice. This reporter, Stone, meant nothing to me, but I had come this far, and I wanted to see the end. Little did I know that the end was nearly three decades away and that I would alternately love and hate this man that lay ill in the jungle but never be indifferent to him or what he stood for or what he achieved in the face of unbearable agony.

✟   ✟   ✟

As we approached the place of Jim's containment, neither sleeping, nor eating, nor communicating except with our eyes, Reena became less and less wary, and I more so. She had prepared herself for his death, and that was the only thing she feared, not the hands of his captors or the puzzle of Hahlos being escorted out under armed guard. I never longed more to hold her in my arms, to possess her, to feel her radiance shine from my own heart. The care she had for this stranger transformed me in those remaining hours. Though I was bone-weary and stumbling the last few miles, her courage drew me with her, defiant and unafraid, into the camp of the Vitani.

White

✦ ◆ ✦

The indecipherable land was marked by contrasts as diverse as the color of our skins and the desires of our hearts. There were miles of savannah and then a refuge of forests and occasional stretches where the canopy closed over us, shielding us from the stifling sun, giving us water and places to hide. We felt safer in the forests but not with each other. We talked less and sat farther apart by our small fires. I had always been at ease with blacks but not with that handsome, complicated man. Our goal kept us together and kept us apart. I felt changed in some incongruous way.

A change had come over Dakimu, too. He seemed to gain strength from a purpose different from mine, matching my strides down the faint path to another cabalistic village, no Huzuni, for sure. I had left my village, that known refuge. I had abandoned it and the people in it who loved me and trusted me and fallen under the spell of Jim Stone. The spell of God seemed a thousand years away.

"Dak! Wait!" I cried, grabbing his arm to slow him down. "We must plan. What will we say?"

"If he is alive, we will try to get him released. If he is dead, we will try to save ourselves," he answered solemnly.

We had no time for more words, for in that instant, we were descended upon by hundreds of masked, ebony giants, the menacing puppets of the *mfalme*, King Kisasi. Hahlos had whispered that name to Dak as they passed on the road. The blacks surrounded us, seeming to come from nowhere and everywhere, seeming to know we had crossed the boundary of their territory before we knew it ourselves. Our wrists were tied and our lips sealed and a mark burned on our left arms in the sign of a cross. When the fire ate into my flesh, I remembered Colonel Hahlos shielding his eyes with his hand, a fiery, ragged cross gleaming from his bare arm through his sweat. And now, we, too, were branded with that mark. Dakimu looked at his torturer with surprise, but his color did not make them any less vicious with him.

We were thrown together in a small, unsheltered pen for cattle and goats. It was filthy, and the sun was oppressively hot. There was no water. Soon the king himself was carried to us on a jeweled throne, borne by twelve natives who stared blankly at us when the *mfalme* motioned for them to set him down and open the gate. We could not get up, so he studied us from his advantage some six and one half feet above. He took each of our arms in turn but not to welcome us. To finger the mark seared there and grunt with satisfaction. Then my mouth was freed but not Dak's, and he said to me in perfect English, "What do you want?"

"Mwanamume eupe! Rafiki eupe!" The white man, my friend! I answered in his own language.

He towered ever closer, astonishment in his eyes.

"Ah," he said at last. "Jim Stone."

"Yes."

"He is ours," the king stated matter-of-factly and began to retreat.

"He is mine!" I screamed, and he turned back. This he understood.

"His woman?"

"Yes."

"You wish to see him?"

"We wish to save him."

"Good. We also wish to save him, until he is of no use to us. You may do what you can. Who is this peasant?" he asked, kicking Dak in his burning arm.

"He may tell you himself," I said, hoping they would unbind his lips.

But the king ignored Dakimu and commanded his men, "Take her to the white man. Remain outside the door. Do not speak to her!"

I was handled roughly and dragged a hundred yards or so to a thatched hut much like the ones Jim and I had watched being demolished from the sky over Huzuni. I was so afraid of what I would see. My heart was in my throat. And then I was tossed through the door at his feet.

"Jim!"

"Reena ... oh my God, Reena!"

He was pale and thin, but he got shakily to his feet and pulled me into his arms. The embrace was intense, altering. It was a place we had never been and so all the more powerful.

"Reena, Reena, how could you be here? How could you find me? There is a God," he whispered, half-crying, half-laughing.

I could barely speak. He hugged me fiercely. The moment was so right, beyond our brief touches in his dark hallway, beyond even that lovely kiss. The hardships of the whole journey to get to him fell away. We embraced in a place far from God, with the holiest meaning of our lives. We embraced for life itself.

Finally I had to say, "Jim, listen to me. I don't know how much time I have. The jeep! Where is your jeep?"

He looked at me uncertainly.

"Gone," he said. "They destroyed it ... miles from here. We were allowed one thing, but can't ... remember ... where ... what ..."

I looked desperately around the dim room ... and my heart leaped with hope. His camera case! Of course he'd bring that! It was the very reason I had put the last two syringes in a hidden pocket inside the jumbled brown bag before he left. I knew he would hang on to that, no matter what. But I never had the chance to tell him. And among the empty, lifeless rolls of film and lenses, it might still be there.

I moved quietly. The guard stayed by the door. I found that the bag had been searched by enemy hands, but not carefully enough, for in its secret hole in the lining was the chloroquine.

"Jim," I spoke to him calmly, although my body was trembling, "I found the serum."

I gave it to him, making him lie down again, but he would not let go of my hand. I knelt in the dirt beside him, trying not to cry. He was so wounded by the malaria, and I so drained by my days on the trail with Dak that some despair came over me. Hahlos was free someplace back in Dar es Salaam, making his cryptic deals, perhaps arming each side against the other. And I was jammed between the lives of two men, black and white, and perhaps between their hearts as well, in a kingdom that hated us all. Color, nor language, nor promises, nor trinkets were going to get us out of this.

So the hand of Jim Stone in mine became a talisman, a prayer, the beginning of love.

✟   ✟   ✟

A commotion erupted outside. I hid the remaining drugs in the pocket of Jim's rain- and sweat-stained shirt. A black warrior rushed into the hut and said in English, "One hour ... you have one hour. No one will disturb you." And he was gone. Jim was drifting on the edge of sleep, still clutching my hand.

"How can I leave you?" I whispered. "What is the reality of all this? Who will live and who will die?"

A stab of pain shot through my arm suddenly, and I remembered the cross. I turned Jim's arm toward the light from the doorway, and there it was, the mark of the cross, singed into his flesh.

Jim spoke with difficulty, "The king has that done to all the Christians, black or white, to identify his enemies. It hurts like hell, doesn't it?"

"Pretty much," I said. "But Jesus died on that cross for me with nails in His hands and feet. I can't complain."

"I guess I can't complain either. It brought me you, an angel. An angel of God, an angel of Africa, my salvation, my great story ... my love."

He slept, and I watched over him. His face was still handsome, unlined, pale just now from being in his dim prison and being sick, his ash-blond hair graying a little and needing to be cut. I wanted to put my lips on his perfectly shaped mouth, kiss him the way he had kissed me in Dar es Salaam. I knew nothing of this kind of attraction. Was this love? I wanted to lie down beside him, feel his heart beating, listen to whispered stories of his life in Africa, why he had stayed so long, why he seemed to need me with a piercing desperation.

But there would be no chance for that. I was taken quietly, half-asleep, out of the hut, and I don't remember seeing Jim again. I was in the dark woods. It was night. A fire burned close by, and around it sat five blacks, two whose faces were familiar. I fought for consciousness.

"Dak!" I cried.

One of the black heads moved. Another pivoted toward it warningly.

"I will speak," it said in Swahili.

It was the voice of King Kisasi. His massive form rose and came to where I was tied to a narrow tree.

"We are returning you to Dar es Salaam safely ... and alone," he added.

"No!"

The voice cut me off and went on, "But if you come here again, you shall die. If you tell anyone of this, he will die," he said, pointing to Dakimu. "Do you understand?"

"Yes ... Dak!"

"Do not speak to him!"

Dak's head turned again toward me, but he remained silent. I rushed on frantically in English, "There is one vial of chloroquine! In his shirt pocket. Bring him back. Dakimu, bring him—"

A rope slashed my mouth and then tightened around my head so that my words were cut off cruelly. I tasted blood. But I saw Dak nod, imperceptibly, as his promise was given.

✝   ✝   ✝

I don't recall much of the journey. I had to be carried most of the way. All they gave me was water and a few pieces of mango. I was blindfolded during the day and left tethered at night like one of their beasts, unblanketed and ignored. I even tried to talk to them in their own tongue, asking at first why they kept Jim and then why they chose such a violent life, but they remained stony-faced and rigid like the hard-boned black statues of city galleries.

And then I told them about Jesus, using the same words that had won the souls of the blacks of Huzuni. But they laughed and spit in my face, except for one, who came to me shyly a few hours before we approached Dar es Salaam, and said, taking my scarred arm, "This cross that people nailed Him to … is it the same?"

"Yes."

"I don't understand this Jesus, but I do understand that we have done to you what His executioners did to Him. And it is that kind of betrayal, that kind of cruelty, He was paying for with His dying."

"Yes."

"He must have been a very great man … I want to know more of Him."

"The one who brought me to your village, Dakimu, he is a believer. Ask him more when you return."

"I shall," he said, and vanished in the shadowy dawn.

But I could not know that by the time he asked Dakimu about his Savior, the black of Huzuni had forsaken Him and even denied what he had known of Jesus Christ.

After we crossed the Rufiji and drew nearer to the city, I found myself alone. My deliverers had crept away one by one to the safety of the forests. They were invaders here and unwanted. A tourist lorry picked me up on the road, and I sat in silence, although my heart was still racing from the events of the past days. The dawn broke over us, strangers speaking in languages I didn't know, marveling at the beauty of Africa in the morning light. I thought of only one thing, Dakimu's promise. He had said it with his eyes, with his heart, which the embittered old *mfalme* could never see. He had said it with that slight nod of his dark head in the presence of his enemies. *I will bring him back …*

Black

After Reena was so ruthlessly torn from Jim Stone's side and thrust back into the wilderness from which we had come only a few hours before, I was allowed to see the prisoner and was made a prisoner myself with him.

"You will stay here," the king said, unbinding my hands and pushing me into the dank hole of the hut.

I stretched out on the cool dirt floor before I even looked at my companion. Every part of my body ached with fatigue and hunger. I did not expect to live. Yet here was a white man, still breathing, compromised by malaria, and separated from the woman he surely loved.

"Reena …"

The voice startled me. It was steady and calm.

"No … it is I … Dakimu. Remember?"

"Dakimu?"

"From Dar es Salaam."

The name of that peaceful city sounded unreal in the lightless hut of the militants' camp.

"The jeep … you gave us our jeep."

"Yes."

"Reena's gone?"

"Yes, but she is safe. Now I must strengthen you and take you back to her."

"Why … are you doing this?"

"I don't know, Mr. Stone. I've told myself I'm doing it for Reena, but that's not entirely true. I had some feeling for you the first time I saw you."

"When I came for the jeep with Colonel Hahlos?"

"No. You and Miss Pavane passed by me in the street. I had heard of you, read some of your work, yet I misjudged you both. When the colonel spoke harshly to me, you showed me respect, and I regretted my hasty judgment. Then Reena rushed in after you … and I could not even be as kind to her as you had been to me, I had so maligned her in my heart. When I finally realized who she was, a missionary from the village of my youth, my sorrow was greater than my fear of what she asked me to do."

"And what … was that?"

"To follow you."

He was silent then, and I moved closer to him to see if he had fallen into unconsciousness, but his eyes were open, and he gazed at me warmly.

"I remember you … and you brought Reena to me. That couldn't have been easy."

"You have no idea."

Then he asked, "Can we get out of here?"

"I don't know … maybe, but I need to know what happened. I need to know the truth."

"The truth? I am as mystified as you, Dakimu, but I'll tell you what I know. You will have to sort out what is true and what is false."

And he began to reveal the most amazing story, involving nations and men I knew nothing of, and I lost hope with every word, and he much of the strength that the serum had given him. But we were together, black and white. We shared a common enemy, a common fear, and although unknown to him, a common passion … Reena Pavane.

✥   ✥   ✥

He spoke slowly, recalling his own strange journey through this capricious land. Colonel Hahlos would tell him nothing for two days. Why he had come instead of one of his men, why they could speak to no one before they left, why they passed up village after village of peaceful natives, the Tulivu, that Jim was supposed to be interviewing and filming for the *London Free Press*, why they pressed on and on into the heart of Africa, into the land of the Vitani, seemingly without purpose.

Near the end of the second day, he was fighting the malaria. He had tried to hide it, but soon was doubled over with pain. Hahlos slammed on the brakes, grabbed his shoulders, and said, "What in hell's the matter with you!"

Jim begged him to just take his foot off the accelerator and tell him what was going on. That's when he got his first look at the truth ... and it wasn't very pretty.

He continued, almost without emotion, but I could sense that he was under a great strain.

"Take it easy, Jim," I said, and was surprised that I could use his name so casually.

"I'm all right, Dak," he said, and he put his hand over mine where it rested by his side, and I was moved by the sight of both crosses suddenly revealed in the same murky light, blood-red and raw on black flesh, and purple and blue on white.

"Please go on," I said, dreading what I would hear.

✛   ✛   ✛

Then the whole story came out. How Hahlos wanted Jim for more than photographs. How he needed his translation skills and his knowledge of trails. How they were on a mission for a coalition called *The Council for Africa*, whose job was to penetrate the Vitani and deal with them directly.

I felt a shiver go down my spine. Nobody dealt directly with the Vitani and lived to tell about it. But here they were planning secret aid to the Tulivu, food and weapons, in case the militants would not back down. The idea seemed, to me, bent on pitting blacks against blacks, so in the end there'd be fewer natives for the Council to deal with.

I let go of Jim's arm.

"I'm sorry, Dak, but I don't have any love for these cross-burners!"

"Nor do I, Mr. Stone," I said, formal again, because I could see that perhaps these blacks, as vicious as they were, had been deceived. I knew, before Stone told me, that while Hahlos was inside dealing, Jim would be out rolling his cameras and gathering valuable information on his big, yellow pad.

"I wanted to negotiate and get out," he was saying, "never put film in the camera, you know? But Hahlos assured me that was the most important part of the plan and the main reason I was given the assignment. If the natives betrayed us, we'd have a lot to show about their methods of operation, materials available, and movement of tribes. In the colonel's words, the three Ms. 'You've got to get the three Ms, Jim!'"

Jim admitted to me then that he almost passed out from the pain and futility of it all, that the whole thing made him sick. Apparently Hahlos had countered cruelly that Jim was already sick and he'd better get a hold of himself, because they were in it now. There was no turning back. That day Hahlos had resorted to his "ace-in-the-hole," which to him seemed like out-and-out bribery. The colonel gathered the leaders of tribes beginning to question our presence and our route straight into the Vitani camps. He promised them food, bottled water, rifles, and ammo for information about King Kisasi. The natives always agreed. Then, at first dark, by pre-arranged code, he'd send up three signal flares. Within the hour a chopper from the nearest Air Patrol base dropped carefully packaged supplies, Enfield .303s, and three thousand rounds of ammunition somewhere in the area.

The colonel's and Jim's safe passage was thus practically guaranteed. The word spread like brushfire. Chiefs were waiting eagerly for their arrival in obscure villages. The colonel seemingly enjoyed every minute of it, playing games, laughing at their maneuverability. Jim said he was sick as hell, but that he wouldn't have seen anything funny in it anyway. He was a journalist, not a damn politician.

"Jim … Jim, it's almost over now."

"Over? It might have been. I might have gone out instead of the colonel. I was not important. They wanted Hahlos. But I was almost delirious by the time we got here, so they kept me, and then they were glad. Kisasi cried out for all to hear, 'Send Hahlos out with message to Council … No deal … You play it our way or we don't play at all! You tell the foreign powers, the white powers, *maybe* we end aggression, if, *definite*, they do not send arms to the Tulivu. *Maybe* we let reporter live, if, *definite*, he does not print words or pictures about our Vitani!'

"And you see, Dak, it was better for them that they held me. I might not have survived the trip out to deliver their message. If I don't survive here, it doesn't matter. No one will know, and the deal can still be made. And Hahlos will be anxious to get out and rethink his plan, whether I live or die not being part of it, of course. These blacks are not stupid!"

"Are you just now learning that?"

"I didn't mean to offend you, Dak, by any of this. You asked for the truth. There it is."

"I must ask you one more thing, Mr. Stone."

"Anything …"

"If you do … get out alive, will you print your story?"

"You're damn right I will!"

Even though I knew he spoke in the height of emotion, that he was in truth a reasonable man, a gentle man, and the one whom I was here to save, I found myself increasingly in sympathy with the Vitani. I did not support their aggression. I did not applaud their violence, but I began to temper an alliance with them because of the color of my skin! Would Stone have not done the same? Would he not have chosen Hahlos over me in a crisis? Was he not doing that already by wanting to write the story of these blacks, possibly lying to them to do it, and following the colonel's orders to do it?

"Get some sleep, Jim," I said, not unkindly, but I was glad he could not see the look I gave him when he lapsed once again into unconsciousness. I had to get out of there. What drove me out into the swift African twilight was not his revelations or his deep bond with Reena but his whiteness! I hated myself for that thought, but it was true. He was a white man, and I a black. These were my people! How could I be blind to their history, their dreams?

And yet, I felt sad for the white man in the hut and even envied him.

But in that savage place, I never imagined I could love him. An irony came to mind. Unfamiliar words to Jim Stone, words I was born to believe, words that applied now to the possibly doomed to die, unsaved one. "He that loses his life shall save it." But what gnawed at me was the question, would the reverse be true? "He that saves his life shall lose it?" He that lives now, when he is so close to death, shall he die, later, when he is rejoicing in life? And what if it is a new life, a life in Christ? Shall that protect him from the hand of death? Pondering these things, I came face to face with King Kisasi, standing in the shadows of the late day, and he said in a deep, incalculable voice, "I have been waiting for you."

White

Major John Sommers leaned over his desk in a rage.

"Miss Pavane, I swear to you, I knew nothing of this! Why didn't you come to me sooner?"

"I was exhausted," I said quietly. "I should not be here now, but you are my last hope."

"My child, my child, I should have been your first hope! It is too late now, I'm sure." He shook his head disparagingly.

"What are we going to do?" I asked patiently, though my mind was way ahead of him.

"You … are going to do nothing. You have done enough already. Convincing the best black I had to walk out on his job, a secure, respected position, and go traipsing into the land of the Vitani! My God!"

"Please, Major …"

"Oh, I'm sorry … but I'm extremely upset!"

"Yes, I can see that," I said, and thought, *how do you think I feel?* But he knew.

"Of course, Miss Pavane, it must have been terrible for you."

"It still is, Major."

"Yes, yes … but—"

"Major … just tell me where Colonel Hahlos is."

"I can't do that, Miss Pavane."

"Why not?"

He answered more calmly, "Things are in a very delicate balance. Although I didn't know the full story, I was made aware by higher authorities of certain requirements, one of which was not to hinder Colonel Hahlos in any way or speak of his movements. I followed my orders. I'm not going to disregard them now."

"I don't think it matters now. They don't care about him anymore."

"Hahlos?"

"No … Jim Stone."

"You see? You care about no one except that dime-a-dozen news reporter! You would risk the security of this country for the life of that one man!"

"I have loved him all this time … but never told him."

"Ah, yes, that's where we came in, isn't it? But, Miss Pavane, it's been six months! Can you hope that he's alive?"

"That's all I have left, that hope."

"And what about my boy, Dakimu?"

"He is more probably alive. His skin would save him, if nothing else."

"Do you really believe that?"

"I think he believed that."

"Then neither you, nor he, in spite of his color, know the Vitani very well. They would kill anyone in their path—black, white, or green!"

I stood up, not wanting to lose that hope so soon, and said, "Major, thank you for your time, but I must try someplace else."

"Where?"

"I don't know. I will look for Colonel Hahlos until I find him."

He sighed. "That won't be necessary, Miss Pavane. I will take you to him … this evening. Shall we say eight o'clock? Wear a black dress and a shawl over your head."

"Major, I …"

"Don't thank me yet. You won't like what you hear."

☩　　☩　　☩

I was met by a black car a few minutes after eight at the appointed place. We drove for miles, in circles most of the time it seemed, before we stopped suddenly in a nearly uninhabited part of the French Quarter of Dar es Salaam. I was thrown out roughly, and the car sped away, tires squealing around the first corner. Almost at once, Sommers appeared in the doorway of an apartment building that was totally dark and void of life.

"Come with me, Miss Pavane," the major whispered tensely. "The colonel is not happy and twice refused to see you, but I convinced him he would be interested in your story. Don't make me sorry I brought you."

We went up a long flight of stairs, across a small balcony that looked down on a courtyard choked with weeds and strewn haphazardly with pieces of plaster and wood from the adjoining structure. They were frozen in the white moonlight like street urchins playing "statue" after dark. We came to a rotting door. The major knocked discreetly in a complicated series of knocks, although I wondered who was there to hear, inside or out, and after a moment or two, a gruff voice said, "Sommers? You may enter."

After we were in the room and the door was shut and locked behind us, Hahlos began ranting at Major Sommers.

"John, what is the meaning of this! You were to bring a message from her, not the girl herself!"

"I knew she would do nothing but speak to you personally, sir, so to save time, I have brought her here."

I had to smile when Sommers came to my defense.

"You fool! I will have no one meddling in these affairs!"

"I respectfully submit that she is already a part of this affair and has been for some time."

"Bah!"

"See for yourself, Colonel," the major said, backing away and leaving me exposed, alone, before the angry man.

He had changed very little since that day on the dusty road, his eyes still sunken, his body slack, his mouth twitching nervously, his expression blank, and suddenly I thought that though I had seen him, studied his face surrounded by blacks, watched him conversing warily with Dak, he had never seen me, nor could he possibly have any idea who I was!

"I don't know this girl! What is going on, John!"

"But, Colonel ..."

"It's all right, Major," I said calmly. "I think he will listen to me."

I walked over to him quickly, before he had time to react, and tore his shirt sleeve back from his left arm. There loomed the mark of the cross, bright and terrible in the darkened room.

"How dare you!" he cried.

"Does it give you much pain, Colonel?" I asked bitterly.

He grabbed my arm to push me away, and his fingers found the puffy flesh, the raised mark beneath my own thin blouse. I pulled up the black cloth.

"Go on," I said in a tense whisper. "See for yourself."

He released his grasp as if touched by fire and stared down at my bare arm, bare except for the wild mark of the cross.

"My God ... you were there, too! But how?"

"I was with Dakimu Reiman. He met you two days out of King Kisasi's camp. Do you remember?"

"Yes ..."

"I was hidden from your sight, but I saw you. And Dak and I went on to find Jim Stone. I was returned from there by the Vitani only a few days after you were, but you could not be traced. I have been waiting for some word from my friends. Why are they not back? How much longer must I wait? What conspiracy were they a part of? What have you to do with their lives? ... or their deaths?"

"Those two ... they were expendable ... but I know nothing of their life or death. I was only there to negotiate peace, perhaps bring back a few photos. I was on a righteous course."

"Then why is there still conflict and killing? Why are two good people still prisoners?"

He shrugged. "Promises were broken. Things got out of hand."

"Whose promises were broken?"

He gazed at me a long time, at my anguished face.

"I have nothing else to say to you," he said with cold dismissal.

"Then God forgive you ..."

"God has nothing to do with this!" he blurted, and he gestured at Sommers to remove me.

✛ ✛ ✛

I found my own way back to the room where I had been living, with Jim's dusty old typewriter and his myriad stacks of journals and newspapers from all over the world that carried his name and his pictures someplace inside. I could hardly bear to look at all those things, the table where we had eaten and spoken of our dreams and what had brought us there and kept us there, the hall where he had kissed me, and the window where we had gazed out, content and safe, where we had not had the chance to say good-bye, where I stood now with emptiness and longing.

I held on to the memory of that short hour in the camp of the Vitani and the promise of Dakimu Reiman to bring Jim back to me, and I let a little of God go out into the African night.

Black

"You know, if the girl speaks of this, you and the white man shall die?"

"Yes."

"And you trust her?"

"Yes, Mfalme."

"Strange ... strange things come of these Tulivu people ... and these missionaries!" he cried with disgust.

Then the king gentled.

"But I like you," he said. "You are like my own son, who was killed only this past month, and his memory is still strong within me. You are more refined, it is true," he whispered, caressing me with his eyes, "but beneath that sleek exterior, that well-schooled mind, beats a savage heart! Am I not right, my son?"

I could not answer. I did not know what he wanted of me. And the king did not behave now as he had in the stockade.

Almost as if he heard my thoughts, he said quickly, "They never should have thrown you in the pen! They should have recognized your grace, your nobility. I would recognize it, if you so choose. I could make you a *jumbe*, a chief, put armies at your command, whatever women you desire. What do you say?"

He held my arms with great tenderness, and I shuddered at his touch and at his next words.

"This mark, my son," he said, fingering the festering cross. "It can be eradicated."

"No! ... No!" I cried, tearing my arm away, but he seemed so disappointed that I tried to explain, to pacify him.

"Not yet, Mfalme ... perhaps someday. I am not ready."

But I knew then that I longed to be free of the mark. It bound me to the whites. It bound me to the Christ the whites loved so, to His promise and His pain, and so I said to King Kisasi, "There is something I must do first."

"And what is that?"

"I must take the white man safely away from here."

"A questionable thing ..."

"Yes, but I gave my word."

"And when have they kept their word?" he said with rising anger. "You would risk your life, your noble black life, for that white dog? Bah! Bah!" He spit out the words and turned away in disgust.

"I shall come back to you!" I called, my heart pounding.

"Is this to be our covenant then? His life, his freedom ... for your life, your devotion to me?"

"If that is your wish, Mfalme."

"It is fair ... although your life is worth a hundred of his! I will agree. It seems that you can be believed, from your loyalty to the white man. Surely you would thus be one hundred times that loyal to me!"

"I shall come back," I said softly.

"And the mark shall be destroyed!"

And with that exclamation, he strode off, satisfied and unassailable, into the blackest of nights. In that moment, I did not know who I was. I lay on the red earth in a fitful sleep until dawn.

✝   ✝   ✝

I awoke with a start. The sun blazed in my eyes, newly opened from darkness, and I shielded them with my hands. They trembled still in the breathless morning air. All around me, men were working, carrying wood and freshly speared game and pots full of gruel back from the central fire to their separate huts. The women were coming up from the river with full earthen jars, singing and laughing. It all seemed so peaceful, I forgot where I was. Could these be the Vitani, so feared and hated? A black stooped beside me in the dust and pulled a good-sized boar leg from the wooden skewer where it had been cooked earlier. I thanked him, and he pointed toward the prisoner's hut and commanded, "You share ... with the white man."

I said yes with my eyes, but my heart rebelled. *He takes my food. He takes my love. Oh, God, forgive me, I don't know who I am!*

I opened the door and said his name. "Jim."

"Dak ... I was worried about you," he said, extending a hand toward me.

In the dim light, we were both the color of gray.

"I was just outside," I said.

"I guess I'm not much of a cellmate!"

"It wasn't that ... I just wanted to be alone."

"I understand," the white man said.

"Do you?"

"Sure. There are some things you can't sort out with people around. Did it help?"

"No ... but something has helped you."

"Oh ... I don't look half-dead?"

"You look like you could get up and walk out of here," I said, truly surprised.

"I'm ready," he said, rising to his feet.

"Hold on, Stone. We can't just saunter off in broad daylight. Besides, do you feel as well as you look?"

"Hell, no."

"Are you hungry?"

"For that?" he said, indicating the barely cooked animal part hanging from my hand. "I don't think so."

"It does look rather gruesome, doesn't it?"

"Do you think they'd let me go down to the river for water?"

"No, I do not! I'll get you some. The *mfalme* is liable not to like you so healthy."

"They'll let you, but not me! Well, color has its advantages," he said with a wry grin and such genuine good humor that I could not be angry.

I said in the same vein, "I don't think my color would get me clear to the river! I'll ask the first black man I see to fulfill your request."

"They shouldn't be too hard to find," he retorted, and I went out smiling in spite of myself. He had done me no harm. Only his color offended me. His heart certainly had never done so, and I was glad I was going to keep my word.

I went in search of the precious liquid. I knew Jim was in need of water and was only feeling so good-natured because of the medicine. *I should give him the other shot of chloroquine. Then at least, he'd have a better chance. But first, the water.* I didn't get very far. The guard stopped me gruffly. Ah … there was a difference! When I was with the white man, I was a prisoner, not the son of kings!

"We need water," I said calmly.

"Maji! Maji!" he called instantly to a passing girl-child, and she stepped over demurely and handed him the jug filled to the brim.

"That is too much," I said.

"You will use it, if he is recovering," the tall, black guard said.

And he was right. That day, Jim could never get enough water. I didn't attempt the shot until the next day. He was eating bits of fruit and the most well-done pieces of meat that I could tear off the scrappy bones they threw us. The next day, he was moving restlessly around the hut.

"Dakimu," he said, "I owe you."

"Just say you will not print a word about our life here."

"That is the only thing I can't do! It's my job; it's my whole life."

"But not the end."

"The end?"

"Of your life."

"The end? You mean the purpose? The meaning?"

"It could be taken that way …"

"It doesn't matter how I take it, Dak. How did you mean it?" he asked.

"I don't know, Jim. I'm not really thinking straight … forgive me."

"Forget it … I'm going to tell you literally anyway. The end, the final purpose, the ultimate meaning in my life is Reena!"

"I'm very glad."

"Is that all you are?"

"You know it isn't, but I am content. I have another end."

"What is it?"

"I cannot speak of mine … yet." I gazed down at the cross on my arm, and he completely misunderstood.

"You're going to spread the Gospel, like Reena?"

"No, Jim … but I can't explain it to you."

"Color again, huh?"

"You might say that."

"Then it is you who should forgive me, Dak."

"Why?"

"For being white and unable to comprehend another man's dream, because he is black. For that, I am truly sorry … Where were we, anyway?"

"The story … the truth you must print at all costs. Would you give it up for Reena?"

"You bet I would!"

"I shall remember that," I said, but not until one, long, agonizing year had passed and I had grown to love him.

✝   ✝   ✝

One day soon after he had survived the second shot at my insufficient hands and the guards were allowing him to walk out from the village for water and a change of scene, although he was always accompanied by a silent black, I said to him, "Sometimes I think you have a black heart."

He had just comforted a crying child, a small girl who had dropped her clay jug full of the morning's water. A piece of the heavy jar had cut her foot, but her tears were not from pain. She could not bear to disappoint her mother, who was patiently awaiting her. He told her in her language that he would get more water quickly, so her mother would not worry, and he picked up an abandoned urn and rushed off toward the river.

He did indeed return swiftly, and patting the child on the head, watched her toddle away with the odd-shaped pot, splashing water in her path. And that's when I said those words.

"I accept that as a gracious compliment, Dakimu," he said, resting his hand briefly on my shoulder and staring directly into my eyes, and I fought not to be moved by his gesture, as I had done so many times before.

✝   ✝   ✝

The days passed, serene, sun-blessed days before the coming of the long rains. There was no word from the Council for Africa, and the Vitani prepared for war. The king left me to Jim, to my first promise, knowing I would keep my promise to him on another day, knowing I carried his arm-cross with me, knowing I would not forget his words in the shadowed meeting place.

It began to seem that the traitor Hahlos and his conspirators had no use for Jim or me. But then neither did the armies of Vitani striding around their camp with renewed purpose. They placed us in the same class. We were outsiders, intruders. We were the same color, foreign. Only King Kisasi recognized my secret bond with his tribes, my equality with them, but he never let it show.

I found that I was walking such a thin line in this complex native existence. I protected the white man, made sure he got decent food and fresh water, laid cool cloths on his forehead when his fever returned, held him through terrible bouts of pain. Then I was the enemy. But when I taught a few blacks to read or helped mothers with unruly children or carried wood for elders, I was the black friend.

But who was I really? The child of a God I could no longer see, even in the beauty of the lush landscape or in the faces of my black brothers? The ally of the enemies of that God ready to do unspeakable things to people that had been my friends?

But Jim, also, considered me his ally and assumed that I trusted him and desired his friendship. And it was true that he was the only man I could really communicate with on any meaningful level. Whether in conversation or lost in distant silences, we were still close somehow, until that inevitable day when he began his betrayal of all that we had been.

I came upon him, his back to me, loading his prized Rolex with color film. I would have slipped from sight, but it was too late. He heard me and turned around, his eyes darkening.

"Dak! Let me explain ..."

"I don't want to hear it."

"Please!"

My heart was steeled, but I listened. That was always my mistake. I gave him a chance.

"I have to do this, Dak. Not for the CFA, not for the *London Free Press*, but for me, Jim Stone. It's in my blood, as much as these war chants are in yours! I need to record these scenes for myself. There are some wonderful shots here, irreplaceable. I will never be back!"

"You may never leave!"

"I'll take that risk," he said.

"Not with my life, you won't!" I said furiously and reached over to smash the great, black lenses, but he barred my way.

"You'll have to break every bone in my body," he said.

"All right," I said with a new and inscrutable demeanor, and I walked out of the hut, jamming my fists in my palms. *There are other ways,* I thought, *other ways!*

It was the beginning of the break between us, although I made one more bargain with Kisasi to save Jim's life, which I don't believe he ever knew. But the wound that was cut that day was never quite healed for all he sought its remedy. The dye was set that stained us black and white again.

At first I didn't see him take a picture. I didn't see him write a word on his notepad. I never noticed him walking where he should not walk, but he knew, he knew what was happening here and why, and that knowledge slowly drove the wedge between us. For it was obvious the Vitani did not mean to wait, if they had ever meant to wait, to keep their part of the deal they had made with Hahlos.

Oh, they were not actually attacking anyone, but day after day, they forged hundreds of spears with poisoned tips, and week by week they collected arms from the Tulivu camps below, camps like Huzuni, now long vanished, and Ngarambe, the home of my cousin who was a farmer. You think these villages had no arms? From one of them, three miles from Huzuni's burial ground, came eight rifles with the seal of Great Britain! Of course, I could have explained the presence of those particular Enfields, and so could Jim, but we both realized the futility of that. We would not be believed.

The final blow came the day the black raiders threw down at the feet of King Kisasi two automatics marked Republic of France, and a week later ten US Army M-1s. I gave Jim Stone a withering look, and he followed me away from the clearing where the weapons lay, a testimony of betrayal gleaming in the sun.

"Dak! Wait!"

I stopped but did not face him. He pulled me around but could not meet my eyes.

"Dak, I don't know what to do," he said helplessly.

"Why don't you take a picture!" I said bitterly.

"Yes, of course! That's just what I'll do!" he said with a trace of sarcasm, and he went off toward the hut defiantly. When he came back a few minutes later, he had the camera bag over his shoulder.

Well, this is the end, I thought with satisfaction. *They'll never allow that.* But I was wrong. The blacks were fascinated by the cameras, and I wondered if these really were the first pictures he had taken, and my heart relented some.

When he passed me by again, he said, "I, too, am appalled by this. Why do you blame me?"

"It is your countrymen, not mine, who have sent these guns, these bullets that shall kill my people!"

"Since when are they 'your' people? I thought we were both victims in this."

"But you are white."

"With a black heart—remember?"

"Even so, you are now their enemy," I said impatiently, taking in the whole village with the sweep of my arm.

"Then why don't they kill me?"

"There is a reason …"

"You know … what is it?" he asked, emphasizing each word.

"I cannot say."

"What about these?" he cried and grasped my cross-branded arm with the one that bore his mark. "Does this not make us alike, Dak?"

I twisted away, the ruined flesh aching from the touch of the white man or from some agony of its own.

"For a little while, Jim, only for a little while longer."

But that "little while" turned out to be the year that I spoke of before. During that time, conditions changed rapidly. The secret mission Colonel Hahlos had been so intent on meant nothing to the Vitani. They did not care to make deals with anyone, black or white. Deals, to them, were threats. So they continued to make and steal more weapons and kept right on with their raids into the peaceful villages. They hated especially the Christian tribes, killing them or luring them back to their camps, branding them with the cross.

The Vitani escalated their minor invasions toward a violent and irrevocable end. The peaceful blacks were not peaceful anymore, with arms from the Council. They fought back and well. The king's troops came in wounded and bleeding and dying. After all, spears are no match for machine guns, even outdated ones! And the weapons the Vitani stole were useless without ammunition. What few rounds they collected in their nightly raids and on the battlefields were gone within the first month. But King Kisasi's cunning could not be matched. From the masses of refugees, he won over recruits to his outrageous cause, with promises like the ones he made me. The sight of his expanding army marching down the valleys was enough to overwhelm villages without a shot being fired.

Then a new phenomenon, the most terrible of all, began to mark the character of Kisasi's revenge: the warriors began to return from battle laughing and whole. The sight of a bleeding man was rare. Jim found out later, I don't know how, but I saw his clear and unmistakable photograph of soldiers killing their own injured and dying before they reached camp, in order to honor the king and not spoil his evening celebration. The picture was entitled *The Means to an End*. Those deaths, of course, were blamed on the CFA, and that, at least, seemed just to me.

Jim began to fail near the end of our time, and I had to seek out the king once more.

"I am afraid for the white man," I told him. "The malaria symptoms are recurring. Can you help?"

"I can, my son," he said. "Of course I have drugs for my people, but for you there will be a price."

"If I can pay it, I will," I said to him.

"I will give you the medicine, and you will marry my daughter. She is pretty enough but not right in her mind. No one wants her. You will take her and make grandsons for me!"

"I will do it," I said, choking on the words.

"So this is how much you love the white man," he said, shaking his head and leading me to the hut of his damaged daughter.

Jim continued to record the brutal details of the tribal wars on his film. I laughed at him, believing the Vitani would never let him go with those pictures. But he fooled us all. For while the war was raging and men's eyes were everywhere but on this unobtrusive, white prisoner, he hid the cameras, negatives and all, in a safe place near the spring where they let him go for water.

One morning, he cursed and complained that his cameras were gone and he must have them back.

"Dak, you can get them. I know you can!" It was quite convincing. Of course, it was easy for me to play into his game—not realizing that it was a game—since I had been so certain all along that they would do this very thing, quietly remove his bulky brown bag in the middle of the night and crush the evidence on the boulders by the river or toss it into the ever-burning fire. He even finally accused me of doing it. He glared unequivocally into my eyes and demanded to know what I had done with his cameras.

"You fool," I said spitefully, "you are better off without them. They might have killed you for them! Forget them. What are they worth anyway?"

"A whole lifetime, Dak," he said sadly. "A whole lifetime."

✛　　✛　　✛

Ah, but it was I who was the fool. For later, when we were set free, he paused not far from camp and turned aside to relieve himself, not bothering to drop his bedroll in the clearing but carrying it with him into the first knot of balsam vines. I thought nothing of it then, but he must have retrieved the bag from his hiding place and rolled it into his blankets, and I remembered later the way he always slept wrapped in one outer layer from his bundle and using the still tight center for a head rest. Oh, the miserable nights he must have borne for the sake of those pictures, those damning portraits of his enemy.

And it was later that I, seeing those photographs in print, came to believe that white men could not ever reach black men on the same plane of compromise or understanding.

White

I stayed six more months after the bitter meeting with Colonel Hahlos. There was violence in the hills, although the worst was yet to come. But no word did I hear of Jim Stone or Dakimu Reiman. It was as if they had never existed. I returned to the dilapidated building where I had last seen the colonel. Both he and Major Sommers had disappeared. But there was a strange figure carved on the door. I put my face up to it in the faint light and recoiled in horror. It was the sign of the cross, crudely and hastily scratched in the rotting wood! My arm ached suddenly, the arm that bore the same mark. I rushed away, agonizing for my friends, both black and white, and that day I bought a plane ticket to the United States of America.

I thought that Hahlos and Sommers were dead, an assumption I held for many years before I saw the colonel again. Every shadow on the street, every dark and silent stranger, every knock on the door was my pursuer, my enemy. I could not sleep. And though I would have been willing to die for Jim and at that time, Dak, too, I could not lose my life for merely carrying the mark of the cross on my arm! It had already been engraved on my soul, the day I gave my life to Christ, and yet I suffered more in the last few months from that place on my flesh than from all the years I'd been a Christian in a pagan land.

I had one hope, and I made one final journey in Africa before leaving the country and all it meant to me. I went to see Rand Healy at the British

Embassy. He was at a great loss to tell me anything, not because he didn't want to, but because he didn't know.

"My dear Miss Pavane," he said, wringing his hands, "I am as upset by this as you are! Jim was a fine man and a personal friend. Believe me, I would do anything within my power to get him back, but I don't seem to have any power anymore! My hands are tied. However, young lady, my lips are not sealed. I am not hiding anything from you. I know nothing of the events you refer to."

I went on, "But the black, Dakimu, from the British Air and Ground Patrol, said he spoke to you the morning Jim left, the morning Hahlos arrived, several hours early, and deceived Jim into going with him on the pretense of some simple, though top-secret, diplomatic mission! Dak said you gave him his orders about the jeep the morning they hurried off without a word to anyone, even Major Sommers, who, it turned out, did know more than he was willing to admit. What am I to believe?"

"You have only me to believe now, Miss Pavane," he said gently, "and I tell you that person was not I! It was someone who used my name, knowing the black wouldn't question it and would follow orders. He knew my name but not my voice. He would do what the voice said. And that is what happened. I am very sorry. And about this Colonel Hahlos. I had never heard he was in Africa or of any council or of any plan to deal with the aggressors. I believe we should just coexist. What else can we do?"

"It appears that someone decided something could be done," I said, with my hopes fading.

"But what? I do not understand any of it. Why was I not consulted? Why was I kept completely in the dark?"

"Mr. Healy, you are a very fortunate man."

"Why?"

"You are alive."

"They may all still be alive, Miss Pavane."

"Yes … but I'm not going to be here to know. I'm flying out today."

"I think that is wise. This country, in times like these, is not safe for a young lady alone."

✛   ✛   ✛

The destination of the plane was Los Angeles. The destination of my heart, unknown. I walked up the littered ramp that led into the giant, sparkling, winged beast that would lift me over the cool, green jungle, over the tangled trails and half-burned huts of the past, over the paths where I was fearless and the paths where I was afraid.

"*Kwa heri* ... good-bye," I cried silently to the rolling sea. *Kwa heri* to the green and red-stained hills. *Kwa heri* to the rushing river that let me live with my black companion for another parting that would take place years from now. *Kwa heri* to all of me that dwelled below, for we were rising, and I remembered rising over the burning village of Huzuni and touching the hand of a stranger. *Jim, were you ever there?* We were pushing against the winds of time that resisted such a parting, that buffeted us among the gray-white clouds of another storm.

I closed my eyes. I saw a small black boy clutching a broken cross. I saw a proud black man wanting to hold me against him. *"Kwa heri,"* I whispered and saw the sweet, loving eyes of Jim Stone ... *Kwa heri,* I wept and saw the angry nails and the blood of Christ in the mark on my arm ... and Africa was a distant, colorless, lifeless realm below.

Black

One night near the end of our imprisonment, the king came to me again and said, "It is time."

I looked into his eyes. They were noncommittal and gray. He was waiting for my response.

"Yes, Mfalme."

"You know what to do."

"I shall return."

"That is all I ask. And you have good reason now. Your wife is with child."

I nodded, acknowledging this new truth, and said, "Do you want the white man killed?"

"Could you do it?" he asked.

"No ... I don't think so."

"His picture boxes must be destroyed."

"That has already been done, Mfalme."

"I see," he said, smiling, and it should have disturbed me then that he thought I had done it myself, when I had assumed that he or his warriors had done it long ago. But there was no time to question him.

"There is a boy who wishes to see you before you go," the king was saying in a low voice. "He was the best friend of my son. But beware! He accompanied the missionary to Dar es Salaam! He was afraid to approach you on his own, so I promised to intercede for him."

"I will see him, Mfalme."

"Raja, you may come forward," the king said, turning to a lithe, brown youth with the medals of three battles around his thin neck.

The boy was excited yet uneasy in my presence.

"You are going back?" he asked softly.

"Yes …"

"Ah, it is good. There is much to learn in other places."

"What is it you want?" I asked impatiently.

"To speak of this man-god Jesus Chreesht."

"Christ …"

"Christ! I shall learn it."

"No."

"I want to know more of the story."

"No."

"She began it, the white girl. She said you would end it for me."

"There is no end."

"What has a beginning has an end."

"The beginning is the ending."

"Did He die for me?"

"You can only die for yourself."

"Can you tell me of His power?"

"There is none."

"And why I must give my life to Him?"

"Never."

"Or why I shall be changed by His life and His death?"

"You shall change more by my life and death than His!"

"You speak in riddles," he cried.

"That's what it is!"

"What?"

"The whole story!"

"I cannot believe what you say!"

"Why?"

"It was such a beautiful story," he said simply.

"But that's all it is … a story."

"Did you not believe it once?"

"Yes …"

"And what happened to your life?"

"I lost it."

"No riddles!"

"I became a good man, I followed orders, I smiled at everyone, I said my prayers, I fell in love with that white girl, she saved my life, and now I am going to save the life of someone she loves! And then I shall return here, to the home of my forefathers, to the place of my beginning without Christ, and I am going to have His mark erased from my arm!"

"It is still a riddle."

"Then why do you ask?"

"To please the girl and satisfy my own curiosity."

"Is it satisfied?"

"No … I do not wish more questions, more puzzles. I desire answers."

"There are no answers."

"You have tried to find them?"

"I have tried," I said honestly.

"Perhaps I could try harder."

"Perhaps … but it takes a great heart."

"That I do not have, and now I am glad!"

"Why?"

"Because the white girl said He loves the least of us the best. Therefore, if He is … He loves me, and that is an answer!"

And he turned his back to me and walked away with a new joy, a joy that I should never have again.

✝   ✝   ✝

Jim was saying good-bye to some children he had come to know and now walked over, ready for our journey.

"What did the boy want?"

"Nothing!"

"Dak, I know better than that. The look on his face made my heart ache. What did you tell him?"

"The truth."

"The truth for you? Or for him, too?"

"You are very wise, Jim Stone, but it may ruin you someday."

"I'm counting on that."

"Why?"

"It will be easier then to love the Lord that Reena so worships."

"Why should it be easy?"

"For faint hearts such as mine."

"Whatever you say, yours is not a faint heart! You don't need Him!"

"Is that what you told the boy?"

"Yes."

"Reena had told all her guards about Jesus, I guess."

"Yes … but I have set him straight!"

"I don't think so."

"Why not?"

"You have not changed that much, Dakimu. You still think of God."

"Only in anger."

"Why?"

"Because He died for me! Why did He have to do that! Why couldn't He let things be! Nobody asked Him to die!"

"But that's why it was such a great gift!" Jim said, surprised at his own words.

"Why don't you let Him take you back then?"

"I will trust you a while longer, Dak."

"But not forever?"

"I don't know. That depends on you."

"I will tell you now. Do not trust me."

"My friend," he said quite seriously, "as long as you have that mark on your arm, we are one. You can change the color of your heart but not the reality of that mark."

"Don't count on it, Jim. Just don't count on it."

"But I shall. I shall, Dakimu. Give me your arm."

"No!"

"Give it to me!"

And he reached out for my reluctant arm and clasped it firmly. The marks danced together in the flickering light of newly laid fires beyond us in the African dusk, and the pain of each diminished in that final touch.

✛   ✛   ✛

The hour of our leaving was set for sundown the following day. Once Jim said, "Do you know where she is, Dak?"

"Reena?"

"Yes …"

"It's been a long time, Jim. Maybe … you won't be able to find her."

"I'll find her."

I had been thinking of Reena, too. How she had looked at me that last time, when they took her away, with those pleading eyes. *Bring him back to me*, they said. And I wondered, also, where she was. It might not have been safe for her in Dar es Salaam. She would be lonely and unprotected. To whom could she turn? Still-living families from Huzuni? She had left them defenseless, unwillingly, but unforgivably in their minds. Major Sommers? She had angered him, too, by asking for my help. The church that supported her in her mission? They probably wouldn't have anything to do with her. She went pretty far off their fundamentalist course.

It was then that I realized, long before Jim, that she had probably said good-bye to the land she loved. She could not wait forever for the one person who cared about her. Would she seek out Colonel Hahlos? My heart lurched at that thought. He would most certainly betray her and even threaten her life, if she got in his way.

I didn't know if it was in that moment that the idea was conceived, but later I decided, with a heavy heart to be sure, that I would save Jim Stone as I had promised, but I would not let him find Reena. I would tell him anything but the truth, whether or not I ever knew the truth. I would take him to England, to his wife, not help him stay and look for Reena or love her on African soil again. This was my country! I would take the invader home and be done with him. I would tell him Reena was dead!

My arm filled with sharp pain suddenly, and I put my good hand over the throbbing mark. I would be free of this! I would not carry His cross. Let the whites carry it. It was not mine to bear.

Jim's arm found my shoulder in the failing light. I could hardly keep from wrenching it away.

"Let's go, Dak," he said softly.

I rose and answered, "I am ready." And we moved out, unhindered, unheralded, into the darkest night.

After he had turned aside briefly a few miles from camp, we did not stop until morning. Then we ate and drank but did not speak for two days. Then, by the crystal pool on the sandy bank where my fierce lips had sought the unyielding white ones, Jim said, "Were you here with Reena?"

"Yes."

"God, I miss her."

"What if she's gone?"

"Gone?"

"From Africa."

"I'll find her," he said. "I will find her."

And he tried to hide the tears that fell in the place where I had almost taken her from him the first time.

"You are a strange man, Jim Stone, but I am beginning to understand why Reena wanted me to bring you back so badly ... now, at the end."

"Our friendship need not end," he said.

"Oh, yes, but it will. We are two rivers with no common springs."

"In the same bed of life, no matter what you say."

"We travel different channels to the sea ..."

"But not in opposition."

"That depends on you."

"How?"

"Promise me you will not print this very story we are living, as I have promised Reena I would bring you safely back."

"That is easy. I have not the means anymore."

And he opened his hands as if to say, "See? No camera, no notebook." He could say that! "I have no means!" While his head rested on the very source of his betrayal. "I have no means!"

I never forgot those words. They haunted me through the rest of our trek together, until I left him on the fog-shrouded English shore, until we met again in that other white land across the sea. "I have no means!" he said. "I shall crucify you!" he meant. And I had no means to retaliate except to hold up to his face the words he might print and say, "See? You lied to me! You nailed me to the cross! For that you must die."

"Dak!"

I met his eyes.

"Whatever you're thinking, let it pass, let it go ... I see murder in those eyes."

"I have not done with killing," I said.

"Is no one safe?"

"No one ..."

"I will remember that," he said sadly, and from that day on, he walked behind me or to one side, but never in front. And it gave me some small satisfaction.

✛   ✛   ✛

African days, African nights, all the same. In with a white girl, out with a white man. I counted the hours. We moved slowly. Jim was not strong, though he pushed himself to his limits, thinking of Reena with every step. I even lifted him once out of the depths of his exhaustion onto the trail again, but he would not give me his bedroll or his hand. He was too close now, too close to escaping with his valuable story. I was so blind.

But the day came when he was blind, too.

"She's not here! Jim, listen, I have been everywhere. No one knows anything about her."

"She was here! In this room! I know that. The scent of her lingers."

We were standing in his old room in the Imperial Arms. Nothing had been moved, he said, but she had been there. He paced the room looking for a sign from her, a note or a scrap of her belongings to give him some hope. Finally, he gripped my shoulders and said, "Tell me what to do, Dak. What else can I do?"

"All right. You won't like it, but I think it is what you must do. Go back to England. Go back to your wife. I'll go with you. I'll see you safely home … for Reena."

"Call the airlines," he said quickly, "before I change my mind."

I sat down at a small table and picked up the phone. On a white pad there was an impression, faintly discernible, pressed there by the hand that had used the sheet before. I could make out only two things, the letters L and A and the number 3. She must have gone over and over the figures. They were quite clear, although I didn't understand their significance yet. L, A, … What did it mean? I could not think straight then with Jim saying, "Why aren't you making that call?"

I hastily pulled several sheets off until the impression was gone, folded them, and stuffed them deep in my shirt pocket. I then began to write on the next clean, white page. *Deception number one*, I thought, smiling shamelessly, and I picked up the receiver.

✛   ✛   ✛

We boarded the British aircraft late that night in the shelter of the moonless dark, unnoticed and alone, and we were grateful. Jim had sent a wire to his wife, begging her silence about his return and asking her to meet us at dawn with a rented car. She would be frantic, he imagined, but would do as he said.

Jim looked terrible in the shadow of the huge plane, as we faced the onramp side by side. I thought he was going to collapse from the strain of waiting and the pain that dwelt increasingly in his eyes, but he controlled himself with a supreme effort and mounted the stairs slowly. I put my hand on his arm.

"Jim, are you all right?"

"No, Dak, I'll never be all right without Reena. But thanks … You don't have to care."

"I don't have to and I don't want to, if you desire the truth," I said quietly, "but I still do, God help me."

He started to respond, but we were being shown to our seats by a slim black stewardess, and he gave up trying to talk to me. Even after we were in the air, he was silent for a long time, gazing out the window at nothing but blackness and the faint outline of clouds in the path of the plane, thinking I know not what about that piece of earth below called Africa. Finally he said, quite softly, with tears streaming down his face, silver in the muted light, freed as the jet from earth, unreal, but there, forever there, those tears, "I'm sorry ..."

✛ ✛ ✛

We were in the air for ten hours, and I reflected on those words. For what was he sorry? Surely not for me, though he carried in his suitcase the means to expose me, to expose my brothers, though he asked of me the ultimate, to stand by his side while he betrayed me. No. It was something far deeper. It was breaking his heart.

Once I said his name. "Jim?"

And he replied, "Don't ask me, Dak. Don't ever ask me."

He was going home ... and I was leaving the land of my birth, my African home of many births—the heathen, the Christian, the servant, the savage. Oh, who was I? I, too, looked down at the continent of Africa that blacks and whites can never both claim. Jim slept, his body spent, his spirit drowning in the loss of Reena Pavane, little did he know. In those few hours apart from earth, my own tears washed my black, illusive face. I remembered Jim's words, "I'm sorry." But it was too late, too late for sealing our friendship. I put my hand on his, as he had done on mine once in the little prison hut weeks ago, but he never knew it was there, and he never heard me whisper in the dark, oppressive air, just before dawn, "I am sorry, too ..."

✛ ✛ ✛

His wife's name was Nadine, and I disliked her immediately. She rushed toward us, all arms and stiff brown hair and darting eyes and whining voice.

"Jimmy, Jimmy, my poor baby! What have they done to you?"

She dismissed me with a withering glance.

"Let me see you, oh, you're so thin!"

"Hello, Nadine," he said. "I'm home."

"Yes, yes, let's not talk of that terrible place! But why this car, this secrecy?" she demanded in the same breath.

"You will soon see," he said with a sigh. "Come on, I want to get out of here."

"Not him, too," she whispered, stressing each word.

"Why the hell not? He saved my life!"

"Oh, Jim, you say such dramatic things."

He turned to me and ignored her sarcasm. "Will you come with us, my friend?"

"I think not, Jim, not today," I said, "but I must see you before I leave England."

"You are going back soon?"

"Yes ..."

"All right. I won't question you, Dak. I'll be at the Crestwood Clinic. It's out of London about—"

"I'll find it," I said abruptly and left them to their discordant reunion.

I saw nothing that day but the dewy London streets, the lonely policemen on horseback wandering the cobbled avenues, and white, white faces everywhere. People were friendly enough, but I could not shake my depression, my disillusionment with myself, the contradictions in my heart. I walked about for another day and did not go to see Jim Stone.

I did not go mainly because I wanted to! I was trying to get back that hatred I had for what he stood for, for what he could do to destroy me. But the plain truth was, I missed him. And I felt bad for him having to face that cold, hard woman and that bare, white hospital. And so the moment came when I assumed my way back into his life.

When they finally admitted me to his room, after numerous and ridiculous questions, he came to me with open arms and hugged me like a brother. Nadine sat stiffly on a wicker-backed seat with her haughty countenance freshly made up, her polished fingernails tapping restlessly on the hardwood arm of the chair.

"Nadine, I don't think you properly met this young man. Dakimu Reiman, my wife, Nadine."

I held out my hand, loathing the nearness of her narrow white fingers, but she ignored the gesture and looked straight back at Jim.

"I know who he is," she said. "Of course, Mr. Reiman, we are very grateful to you. Now, if it's money you want ..." She was opening her purse, but Jim reached over and snapped it shut.

"Nadine, for God's sake!"

"Oh, Jim, that's all these people want."

"Get out of here, Nadine. You don't know what you're saying."

"I think I must stay," she said coolly.

"Why?"

"The doctor said you weren't to be disturbed by visitors."

"You are disturbing me greatly! I want to talk to this man."

"So continue," she said calmly.

"Without your interference, Nadine. I mean it."

"Have it your way," she said, indifferent now, and stalked out without ever having met my gaze.

"Now, Dak, where have you been?"

"Here and there, getting the feel of the country."

"And?"

"And I was not too displeased ... until I came here."

"Oh ... Nadine ... you must forgive her. She is quick to judge."

"Of course," I said, hating her even more.

He was facing the window now, silent and withdrawn and maybe even a little afraid of me, and that is when I began to lie ...

"Jim, I have something to tell you. That is why I didn't come right away. I was checking a lead, and it ended ... here."

"Dak, tell me!" he said. "It's about Reena, isn't it?"

"She's dead," I said softly, and the words screamed in the still room. "There's no doubt. I have sent to Africa for documentation, but I am sure."

He had a stricken look on his face. He sat down on the edge of the bed and stared at the floor. I could not see his eyes, but I knew they were flooded with anguish, and the mark on my arm throbbed warningly. Now I was a betrayer … but I could not repent. I could only say, "I'm sorry, Jim. She was killed in a plane crash on her way to England. She must have hoped you would come here, if you were ever released."

"But how …?"

"I found a note in your room, just a scrap of paper. It didn't make much sense at the time, so I kept it from you. Later on I figured out what the letters and the number meant … the name of a second-rate British airline and a flight number. I discovered yesterday … but could not face you. The plane never got here. It went down over the Sudan. There were no survivors."

"My God …"

"I didn't want to tell you … but I had to, you see. There might not be another chance."

"What … are you saying?"

"I am going back to Africa … tonight. I have kept my promise."

"No … Dak."

"You will have proof in a few days. Then you can begin to forget her."

"Never," he said. "She may be dead, but I will tell her story. She will come alive through my words."

"Jim, you cannot! I could never go back to Africa, and I must!"

"It won't touch you, I promise. I'll leave you out of it."

"That's impossible! It is my story, too."

"I'll change your name."

"Everyone would know …"

"Dak! The blacks betrayed the Council, just as they were deceived into backing off on the Tulivu. I know the Vitani were collecting and making weapons long before the Tulivu received any from the CFA. They weren't waiting for any peace talks or secret deals! But I'll show both sides. I have no reason now not to reveal everything."

"No reason?" I spoke coolly through my galloping rage. "There is one reason you have not considered."

"And what is that?" he asked in a broken, barely audible voice.

"Never to take your pen in your hand … to save your own life."

"Oh I have thought of that, Dakimu. I thought of it all the way out of the mountains and all the way home, and I'm thinking of it now, and I say to you, what good is my life without Reena? To write the story will heal me."

"And damn me," I said, and I left him with his pain.

I ran to the nearest telegraph office and dictated instructions into the senseless wire, to a source the Vitani had inside the city of Dar es Salaam, a name given to me at the last minute by King Kisasi. The words read in the cryptic Swahili tongue: FAKE DOCUMENTATION. .DEATH OF REENA PAVANE. .PLANE CRASH EN ROUTE TO ENGLAND. .SEND TO JIM STONE. .CRESTWOOD CLINIC. .LONDON, ENGLAND. .DAK R. And I caught the first flight back to Africa, my left arm exploding where the mark lay concealed beneath my sleeve. It scourged me, mocked me, but I smiled. I had done it … deception number two.

✛   ✛   ✛

Africa had never been so beautiful to me as it was when I landed in the gold and crimson dawn, a reprieve to my eyes after those dreary, sunless English mornings. The sky was cloudless and bright, the blue crashing against my eyes, as I descended from the air to my beloved homeland. And I was filled with another vision. I would find myself again in the heart of the forest, away from the double-edged sword of white men's words. I did not condemn my own falsehood. It had arisen out of their lies. I had only one regret—that a man like Jim Stone, who was basically honorable, had to be the first to fall under my axe of revenge, although he had been the first to betray. It was unconscionable to hurt a man I loved, even though his truth, the story he might tell, could lead to my own death.

I did not stay in the city long. It was too dangerous. I was wanted now by the British Embassy and British Intelligence for "information concerning Jim Stone," the note that was pressed into my hand by a courier as I left the airport demanded. "Urgent" it also stated. *I'll bet*, I thought, smiling to myself, and I was glad he was in England. There he was safe from them, as well as from me. I wondered what the Embassy would do if they knew the whole story, but I resisted an urge to announce his seclusion in the Crestwood Clinic. I walked past the embassy building, the ten blocks between there and the British Air and Ground Patrol base, and saluted the new major, whose name I did not know, and said, "Dakimu Reiman, reporting for duty, sir."

"Good! The new boy!"

Apparently he did not remember the old boy's name!

"Yes, sir."

"They need a jeep up at Station 10. Some injuries reported, nothing serious, but could you leave within the hour?"

"I think so, sir," I said.

It was perfect. He saved me the trouble of evading the police with the stolen jeep until I got it out of Dar es Salaam. I took the hour to check on the report sent to Jim Stone. It, too, was foolproof. My contact had used the name of an airline that had lost several planes in the last year. The dates were confused and the news coverage scanty. The company had paid plenty to play down the incidents, I was sure. One of the victims of a terrible crash in the north of Sudan was a lovely girl, whose faded picture in the African paper had no name in print and resembled Reena startlingly. I stared at it amazed, and my heart had a wild, dizzy moment when I wondered if it was really her. But no! Her scratch pad had said LA, and I had finally determined that to mean Los Angeles, California. She had not even thought of going to England!

I filled the jeep with British supplies and arms and headed west, taking a longer route to avoid crossing the river where Reena and I had been lashed together and survived. I felt empty when I thought of it now. The further place had a friendly, well-maintained bridge. I wanted nothing to separate me again from my goal. The jeep ran well, and I laughed at the havoc that must be reigning now at British Headquarters. Station 10 was in the other direction, and by this time, they would know that I had never reached that outpost. *Deception number three, nicely executed*, I thought, as I moved securely along the deserted, dusty road.

✛ ✛ ✛

It was a joyful drive this time into the wild country of my birth, of my blackness. For the first time, I savored the meaning of that color. I called out, "Hello, brothers!" to all I met. But the peaceful ones turned aside, and I canceled them out in my mind as white men's tools. The whites could not use me anymore! "Drive faster, Dakimu. Don't forget to pick up the major at seven sharp! That jeep needs a lube, Dak." And on and on, an endless list of servitude and courtesy to men who dealt now behind my back. And now, I shall deal behind their backs!

They knew I was coming, the savage ones, the Vitani. Secret trails were opened up to me to hasten my return. Food was given freely, bows of respect as I passed their camps. I was the Prodigal Son. But the strange thing was the name they called out ... "Alama!" ... Sign! My identity now lay in the mark on my arm. "Look for the cross and let him by," was the watchword of the fiercest and the lowliest. I was the hope of all, with my city knowledge and my native heart. I never heard "Dakimu" again in the camp of the aggressors.

Even when King Kisasi greeted me in his village at the end of my exalted passage, he said, "Alama, my son!"

"I am here, Mfalme," I answered.

"You have kept your promise."

"Did you not believe I would?"

"I did not doubt, but the sight of you confirms my dreams. You are a man of much honor. You must serve me."

"I shall never leave you!" I cried with passion.

"No! Do not promise that ... There will be a time."

"Never!"

"When the war is over and your mark is removed and I am gone, there will be no need for you to stay."

I hung my head. The old king was right. I could not stay forever. I had other tasks to accomplish, in another world, where my black face would not be so welcome, where I would be hated instead of loved.

"I await your orders, Mfalme."

"Tomorrow," he said gravely, "we begin the massacre! You shall be my advisor, command all my troops and sit at my right hand."

"Yes, Mfalme."

I thought of Reena, wherever she was, not believing I would agree to such a thing.

"We will send runners toward the city to blow up ammunition sources," the king was saying. "You know these sources?"

"Yes."

"Good!"

"Deception number four," I muttered.

"What did you say?"

"I was counting how many … There are four storage houses …"

"We shall kill the leaders of the Council, if they can be found. Then we shall be ready!"

"Ready?" I asked, incredulous. "Is that not enough?"

"No, my son. Then we shall invade the Tulivu villages, clear to the edge of the city! To the heart of Dar es Salaam! The haven of peace shall be the stronghold of the Vitani! We shall hold every tribe hostage with the very weapons the white man gave them! Is it not just, my son?"

"It is just."

✛   ✛   ✛

Yes, it was just, but it was bloody. May I never live to see such a massacre again. And my part in it? Ah, the black men who were killed because of me, the white men who were murdered, the children who begged for mercy and were slain. The cause was just. But the means? The means to that end far more of a betrayal than Jim's photographs inside his bedroll! A hundred times more vicious and unforgivable. But I gloried in it, though day and night my arm raged with fever, the mark blistering and boiling and yet goading my heart even more into the thick of the battle. And when the palms of my hands dripped with blood, my own red river mingling with that of brothers and enemies alike, I remembered the nails in the hands of Christ and knew the pain He bore, and in those rare moments, honored Him again …

The days became weeks, and the weeks months, and the killing did not cease. I, with my own hand, slew John Sommers in the streets of Ngoma, a Tulivu village close to a BAP station. He was unloading guns, and I called out his name. He turned, and his face went whiter than the white of his skin, and he cried out, "Dakimu, not you! No! Not you!"

And he dropped the weapons and faced me, defenseless and terrified. "You cannot have done this!"

"This! And more!" I screamed and rammed my knife down his throat and left him choking in his own blood. I killed three more who had run to aid him, a black and two whites, with no emotion. I charged across field after field, under the name Alama. And still I did not know who I was. I fought on.

But I did not die. I braved the darkest rivers and came up unscathed, as I had from the river of my abjuration with Reena Pavane. And if she could see this madness and this glory now, would she wish she had let me die in that flood-swept Rufiji years ago? Could she have loved me enough then to rip me now from the side of King Kisasi?

Ah, Dakimu, you are gone at last, and in your stead stands Alama, and though your flesh shall soon be cleansed of that old wound, your soul is marked by that dark cross, by that one death. Too late, too late for you to know His truth. You bear the sword of the angel that fell from heaven to wield his own black power. Hah, Satan! Even you have never known this! And I chopped off the heads of three white children gazing up at me from their God-blessed beds in utter disconsolation.

White

✧ ✦ ✧

The children were not afraid of me, as the black children of Huzuni had been on the first day. They greeted me as if it were a normal occurrence to have a stranger in their midst.

"Good morning, Miss Pavane."

"Are you our new teacher?"

"Will you be here for a long, long time?"

"Would you like some hot chocolate?"

One black face stood out in the curious huddle of new faces. I smiled and tried to answer their questions and then found myself staring out the window of the adobe schoolroom.

The land was as empty as my heart, little green to soothe the places in me that needed Africa to survive. I had seen my mother and father briefly in La Puente, California, where they had established a New Life congregation and still preached the same "everyone is a sinner" story to people who could not imagine a Christian like Dak or a nonbeliever like Jim Stone. So many wasted words, so much judgment made me yearn for Dar es Salaam. I moved to Taos soon after an awkward few days trying to reconnect with my past, but I ran from that like Nathan had run from me in the clearing at Huzuni. *We're all running from something*, I thought. The only thing that stops you in your tracks is love.

La Casa de la Paz merged with the rolling red-brown hills, its clay buildings and white fences spread out across fifty acres of New Mexican plain. The House of Peace, its name translated from Spanish, meant just what it said. All faiths were welcome there. No child was refused because of color or "sin." There was one rule: do unto others … They didn't have to be baptized or speak in tongues. They didn't have to believe God was a magician or that He answered every prayer. They were allowed to ask questions, about their bodies or about the universe. The library was filled with books of poetry, science, history, and, of course, the Bible, but the Bible wasn't considered the only source of truth. It was true enough for most of them. They loved the stories of Jesus just as my African children had. They wore crosses around their necks, but I was careful that they never saw the one on my arm.

Most of the youngsters were orphans. They had names like Elena and Maria and Stephen and Gallis. They were offspring of drunks and drug addicts and accident victims. Most had suffered some kind of abuse. Most would never be adopted. They called La Casa de la Paz their home.

It soon became my home. The desert had its delights and its secrets, little water to swim or drown in, amazing sunsets with all the colors of Africa streaming out across the sky. I was not lonely. But I was not complete. The Christian dogma that had given my life meaning got caught in the dry wind and tumbled away. What I wanted was what I had felt in Jim's darkened hallway, his hands holding mine against his heart.

Africa was where I had lived for life itself. New Mexico would be a transition to a life lived for others, or so I thought. I would come from the classroom and pick up Jim's picture, one that I had cut from the magazine beside his first story about Africa. My week and one hour with him was the only thing that felt true. Loving the children was easy. I craved something hard, something that demanded my whole heart, although half of my heart was missing. The mark on my arm flung me daily between two worlds, the truth of the cross that soothed the lost of La Casa de la Paz and the truth of the cross that branded me as a betrayer of Africans. It was a story Jim Stone would have loved to tell.

Black

✧ ◆ ✧

The ceremony had begun. The massacre had ended. All around us the country lay torn and bleeding and finally at rest. Some even called it peace. And we, the aggressors, the undefeatable Vitani, were celebrating our victory … dancing and feasting and making love and drinking and dancing again. Many men had died, and many women were lonely, and yet there was no time for sorrowing over lost lovers or sons. The women cooked and bandaged and let us make love and joined in the dancing now and then.

The king was very happy. He smiled from his huge gilded throne and took part in everything as he was able. He clapped my back and cried, "Because of you, my son, we have demolished the betrayers!"

I smiled, but I was full of bitterness. *He does not know Jim Stone! He does not know the words he can write.* I still did not know of the photographs he could print! But I was blind no more. Both sides had betrayed, and both sides had paid the price, except for Jim. Oh, I had denied him Reena. That part pleased me. He suffered her loss. But I suffered, too. I was dead inside. I could not celebrate, except for the outward show. I had killed so many; one more would not matter. Then perhaps I would be free.

My arm twitched, and I grimaced. *Yes! That, too, I must be free of! That mark! That unholy cross!*

The king looked down.

"Soon, *mwana*, my son," he said, "when the singing is finished."

109

They sang for three days. My head was spinning, my heart drunk, when finally Kisasi stepped down from his throne and raised his hand. The silence was stark after the tumult of the chanting and the pounding of naked feet on the hard earth.

"It is time to make Alama a brother. He has earned the title well. Now he must bear the final test, the test that no man has endured, the purging of the mark from his arm!"

The crowd gasped and shrank back, suddenly awed. I was going to suffer that? I was not sane to suffer that!

I shouted at them, swinging my arm wildly through the air, revealing the crudely hacked cross on my quivering, black skin. "It must be removed! I shall not bear the mark of the white man anymore!"

Then they yelled their approval, *"Kuondoa! Kuondoa!"* Remove! Remove!

A young black thrust a smoldering branch into the fire, and it leaped into flame. He carried it to my place by the king and waited with the rest, silent again and expectant.

Kisasi turned to me and said, "It is your choice, *mwana*. Who shall do it?"

And I flickered not an eyelid, trembled not a limb, when I said, "You, Mfalme."

And he reached for the torch.

Fire, water, fire, water, so my arm itself would not burn, he stripped the mark. He made deeper scars and wilder lines and left a mottled cobweb of black and red and white upon the place. It was as if a carpenter had chopped the rugged cross to splinters on my flesh. I screamed for all the betrayals, even my own, for the loss of kinsmen, for the loss of Reena and Jim, until I fell, screaming still, upon my molten arm, where the cross of Christ lay broken there at last.

I woke at dawn on the second day, and at first remembered nothing. I did not feel ill. Why was I lying there with King Kisasi hovering over me?

"Mwana?"

"Mfalme?"

"Now you are really my son," he said gently, and he touched the wounded place where the cross had been, and I remembered. I looked at it ... only an odd, white, mangled symbol met my eyes, and then he said, "The skin will never be black again."

"That does not matter! The real mark is gone, the cross I could not bear."

"Yes, you are free from that forever."

I closed my eyes for a moment, and when I opened them again, he was gone.

✝   ✝   ✝

The aftermath of battle was always a hard thing. The days began to drag, our muscles softened. We laughed and slept and dreamed, and then we became restless again. For the natives, there were children to train, crops to tend, huts to repair, fires to kindle. For me, there was nothing. My simple wife had given birth to a girl-child, and she sat all day in our bridal hut rocking and singing to her the same tune over and over. She did not interest me anymore.

Because she was the king's daughter, she had many servants and did not have to mend or cook or bring water from the river or even dress herself. The baby was handled by other maids. There was no work for me to do. I began to retreat into the cool, dark forests and dream of the battle-days and festival-nights. And for a while, I enjoyed this time alone, this peace within the hills of the Vitani. But there came a time when I wanted more. I was not finished with war. I longed for conflict. I could not connect to anything else. I needed to feel my blackness thrown against whiteness, to charge the world that my blackness had been compromised by whiteness. But I waited in silence. It was not yet time.

And then, one soft spring day near the end of my seventh year, including the one with Jim, in the camp of King Kisasi, I approached the aging *mfalme* with my need. The old man was frail now, hardly a giant anymore, but he took my hand, as he had done so many times in the past, and he said to me, "Mwana, you have other promises, do you not?"

"Only to myself, Baba."

"You must keep them," he said weakly.

"They do not avail themselves here …"

"I know …" He paused, groping for words. His free hand rose and fell on the pillowed bed. "Have you anything to keep you here?"

"I would stay for you, Baba."

"Your child?"

"She is a half-wit and not mine," I said sadly. "There is no likeness in her eyes."

"Yes … I suspected as much. Well then, you must go. I set you free, Alama! I give you back to the world. Do what you have to do."

"But, Father …"

"The others, those to whom you have promises, they need you more."

"Only to myself have I promises," I repeated slowly.

"I know better, my son. You cannot resolve them here, you cannot resolve them alone. Nenda!"

"Mfalme," I said softly.

His eyes sparkled for an instant, only an instant.

"I will go … with you in my heart," I whispered.

And his eyes shone brighter, deeper, clearer, for one last time, before the light went out of them altogether and the life, and I staggered out of the darkened room into the blinding sun and said to the motionless air and the gathering, silent black people of the Vitani, "Amekufa."

He is dead.

✝   ✝   ✝

I stayed one day in Dar es Salaam, just long enough to learn the location of two men. It was not difficult. Almost everyone knew and thought nothing of revealing the information to a well-dressed black who asked so politely.

"The United States, yes, they are both there."

Colonel Edmunde Hahlos and Jim Stone. Jim had left England because he could not get his book published there. He had written it after all! I still did not know about the photographs, and I discovered the following details in various conversations.

The British government had refused to sanction the memoirs of a man written mostly while in a hospital recovering from some illness that might have affected his mind, whose words would most certainly affect the views of the world on Britain's relationship to the affairs he spoke of. In short, they wanted no part of it or of Jim Stone. He was considered dangerous with his outlandish claims about councils and traitorous civilized blacks and savage kings! He was welcomed with open arms by the United States, who was big enough to bear the brunt of criticism and come out looking like a hero for giving the journalist a chance to exercise his right of free speech, and of course, free press! So there he was, in some US sanctuary, typing away.

Colonel Hahlos was a different matter. This man, in fact, seemed to have many friends. Where Jim was maligned, the colonel was praised; where Jim was avoided, the colonel was mobbed. He was on a speaking tour in the United States, explaining the British position to the American public on African affairs, and they were taking it all in. Oh, he was questioned about the forthcoming memoirs of some insignificant reporter from his country, but he neatly set them aside and went on with his main pitch, which was: Britain had remained neutral before and during the Massacre, gave arms to villages only in extreme circumstances, promoted peace at all times, and never, never lifted a finger to harm a native.

Armed with this information, I sailed again from my dark home shore into the storm-studded sky, into the jungle of lies of another land. I boarded the first plane to the United States, having no idea where to look for my betrayer, my friend. Perhaps if I had, I might have held in abeyance all the forces that were gathering inside. I might have seen my country below, poised on its own healing, radiant in the eye of the sun, defying the troubling clouds, denying my insolence and calling me down again. But I stared straight ahead and said only with my lips, only once, "Africa … *kwa heri!*"

White

The children were hanging around me, reaching out and questioning me.

"I am only going to the city. I'll be back tomorrow, my dears," I assured them.

But they did not understand, for I had never left them like this. And I did not understand myself why I was so intent on going. I had only a scrap of information ... a lecturer from England on Africa, our little newsletter said, nothing more, not even a name. And yet I was drawn as if to a magnet. The children had washed one of the school cars, polished it obsessively for their teacher's big trip.

"Bring me a present!"

"Mail this letter!"

"Call my aunt!"

They all cried out at once.

"Children! Children! I will bring you all something ..."

Sighs of satisfaction.

"Now be good and say your prayers, and I will see you in the morning."

"We will! We will! Tomorrow then! Good-bye!"

"Good-bye ... *adios*. Good-bye ... *kwa heri*." When I said those words in the sky over Africa, I did not return. And now I was saying good-bye in another language with every reason to return, and yet it was there, that small doubt that I would ever see them again.

I drove quickly out of the schoolyard and down to the gravel road, and then I had thirty-nine miles and less than an hour to reflect on the last seven years ...

✢   ✢   ✢

They had been serene years, with joy in giving once more to people who rejoiced in the gift, who accepted my love and my life because I, too, was capable of error and grief and pain. The children were not unwise. They discovered almost at once that I had a weakness, a secret that they could not share. I never bared my arms to the sun. My nightgowns all had sleeves to the wrist, my day-dresses the same, and I always wore them, even on the hottest days.

It wasn't that I was ashamed of the mark. But it was a bittersweet reminder of those other arms that carried that sign, Jim and Dakimu. Hahlos I believed to be dead, but I still had hope for the black and for Jim. The mark held the victory of Christ in its rough-hewn, tissue-scarred lines, but it also was a part of the past, a past I came to La Casa de la Paz to forget, and I did not want to open up that wound.

They did not ask again, those trusting children, far behind me now in the evening's twilight calm, after I had explained that I, too, had abandoned little children just as they had been abandoned, and I wore the sleeves to remind me of what I had done.

"And you came to us, since you could not go back to your other children," said Stephen, the perceptive one.

"Yes ... I cannot love the others again, so I must love you."

"I'm glad," said Eva, with her dimpled smile and innocent way of seeing things.

"I'm glad, too," I said.

"Will you ever be able to cut off your sleeves?" asked the inquisitive Moon-Flower.

"I ... don't know, my child of the Iroquois."

"We will not let you go until you do!" cried the possessive Raphael.

Parting, the one word we did not enjoy at La Casa de la Paz. Parting meant leaving the peace of the house, facing the outside with its pain and loneliness, but knowing you had to ... So to the older children who left, we said:

"Don't cry, Susan Sun. You will be back to visit us."

"Wipe your tears, Manuel. There will be no time for them out there in the world."

"Give me your grief, Elena, for I must stay here while you meet new faces and see the rest of life."

Was this another parting for me, an abandonment of my New Mexican home?

✛   ✛   ✛

The parking lot was full. *He must be an important man*, I thought with rising anticipation. I had to walk a short distance, but I didn't mind. The air was fresh and balmy, and though it was now dark, the streetlights blazed, and car lights flashed in my path, and the whole place seemed like one big stage readying itself for the final act, the last curtain of a great play. And it was almost true, that analogy, for what happened here ultimately sealed us all again under the same sky, on the same square of earth, for our inevitable consummation.

I took a seat in the rear of the auditorium, my heart pounding, my throat dry. I knew! I think I knew, even before he appeared on the distant platform with the appropriate dignitaries and their long-winded introductions, that it would be him. He rose to speak. He was heavier and more weary-looking, and his hair was silver-white and thinning, and his voice was less steady and less angry, but it was the same man! It was unbelievably, but unmistakably, Colonel Edmunde Hahlos.

I suppressed a cry. Alive! Still alive and standing haughtily over this crowd, and I suddenly thought of my father, remembered his way of waving his arms above the heads of the blacks, commanding them to silence before he spoke, weary and gray and haughty as this loathsome man. It struck me then, in the presence of Colonel Hahlos, that perhaps my father had not belonged in that land, that none of us should have asked that dark, unruly

Africa to love us or allow us to step foot on her ancient shores. Perhaps my father and I had been just as guilty of betraying those people when we promised them salvation and glory instead of guns!

"Guns! Believe me," the colonel was shouting, "the peaceful blacks were forced to take up arms to defend their children, their homes. Who would not have come to their aid, I ask you?"

I had not heard anything he had been saying. His face was red and sweaty now, his hands trembling, his eyes dark. He reached for a glass of water and drank it down quickly. The crowd grew restless and impatient. They were not prepared for this man. They had expected to learn of a white man's journey through a black continent, a tale of big game and rain forests and shy natives. This talk of guns and blood and hate disturbed them. These political and moral overtones pricked at their consciences, made them sit up and gasp at every word.

And he used that incredulity to enlist their sympathy, their respect for his part in the drama. He never told an outright lie, but he did not reveal the whole truth. He did not bare his cross-riddled arm or speak the name of Jim Stone. He did not tell of the Council for Africa or of the source of any weapons that ended up in the hands of blacks. He admitted nothing that would destroy his image as the generous benefactor of the downtrodden savages. And if the listeners did not quite believe him, they at least responded to him, and that was all he wanted. He did not really care what they thought of his words. What mattered was what they thought of him, what they would say next week to a neighbor or a friend … "Wow, that Colonel Hahlos, he was a brave man. And what he did for those natives! Fine gentleman, proud to have heard him …"

He talked for two hours. No one moved, and his voice filled the room with renewed power, overwhelming even a sense of reality. Was he talking about Africa? There were no references to actual people or to the secret and wonderful places he had seen with his own eyes. His images were vague and distorted. No one would ever see the faultless beauty of the land or the heartless deception of its people by the white aliens.

Near the end, he said, "I leave you now with this brief and simple picture of a vast and complex nation. I hope my presence here has inspired you to take up arms against the injustices of the world, to deplore the prejudice and racial misunderstanding that abounds everywhere, and to be a force for reconciliation instead of aggression ..."

He paused, as though he was going to say more, but then sat down abruptly with a hurried thank-you, and I felt that his grim look had not arisen out of concern for words already spoken but for words he had been about to say. There was an instant uproar when everyone realized he was finished.

"Question! Question, Colonel!" several voices called to him out of the audience.

He stood up and began to answer the first query cautiously. I only wanted to know one thing, where he had come from and where he was going. What my presence would do to his composure I did not know, but I wasn't taking any chances. I looked at the exits. They were crowded with latecomers, all talking and asking questions. Then, wait, there it was, he was saying, "... and from LA, friends, I'll be returning to my headquarters in New York for an unscheduled summer of rest."

"Will you, also, be writing your memoirs?" someone asked with a hint of sarcasm.

The colonel laughed appreciatively, but the joke was lost on me. All I could hear after that was the name of that city, New York. He was going to New York! And I knew I would go, too. I could think of nothing else. But even then I believed I would return to my life in New Mexico, to La Casa de la Paz.

I tried to explain to Headmistress Maggie Santiago on the phone from the airport, after I said simply, "I'm going to New York."

"Why, Reena, whatever for?"

"I'm not sure, Maggie. But I'll be back. I want to come back."

"Oh, my dear, if you go that far, how will you come back?"

"With my heart, Maggie. At least with my heart."

"We will miss you, Reena."

"And I, you ... always."

"It is really good-bye then, isn't it?"

"Yes, but I didn't know it ... until now."

"The speaker?"

"Someone I used to know."

"I understand."

But I knew she didn't, and I was too impatient to tell her more.

"God bless you all, Maggie," I said finally and cradled the receiver.

✛　　✛　　✛

In the air again, winging with the silver bird of night toward an unknown rendezvous, a victim still of the singing past. I could not let it go, the reality of what had happened in my African home overshadowing all the healing at La Casa de la Paz. My house of peace had been shaken with one blow from that violent past.

I could not sleep, although the passengers on my flight were quiet. I was separate in my wakefulness, in my watchfulness for the dawn that would lead me, ultimately, to the beginning or to the end ...

✛　　✛　　✛

I found a small, secluded room, if one can be secluded in the sprawling city of New York, in a comfortably old and clean hotel ... and waited.

I didn't have long to wait. The colonel followed in a few days, although it was I who was following him. There was a huge crowd at Kennedy Airport and rings of security and blockade ropes and important-looking people trying to talk amid the babble of one indifferently busy terminal. I kept away from the crowds, from the secretive groups of men. My arm trembled under my thin blouse, and I could see the outline of the cross paler than the rest of my skin through the translucent cloth. I wished that I had brought a jacket, although it was not cold.

I had come to see Hahlos. My mind was set on nothing else, my heart closed to any other sight, when suddenly my breath died in my throat and I stifled a cry that would have turned a hundred heads, and I strained my eyes, as the figure darted in and out, shadow-like and illusive through the mass of people. The black head twisted here and there. I lost it, and then found it, closer still! The face was bearing down on me now, aloof, beautiful, disdainful, the same, yet not the same. It had to be him!

"Dak!"

The face stopped, eyes flashed back and forth, lips tightened almost angrily.

"Dakimu," I said directly in front of him, and his eyes met mine.

"Oh my God," he whispered, and before I could speak again, I was in his arms but only for a tense moment, for he led me quickly into some empty waiting room, locking the door behind him, as if he suddenly realized he could not stand there in that crowd holding me, though we were both so stunned by the sight of each other that we embraced again, wordless and filled with emotion.

"Reena! My God, Reena. What are you doing here?"

"I might ask you the same question, my long lost friend," I said half-smiling, but the intensity was still there.

He pushed me away from him but still gripped my shoulders.

"Where did you come from?"

"New Mexico."

"You must go back!"

"Why?"

"This is no place for you!"

I questioned him with my eyes.

"You will see, Reena ..." He paused, and then said, "Only I don't want you to see! I don't want you to get mixed up in ... Oh, what the hell!"

He let go of me roughly and unbolted the door and started out toward the crowd.

"Wait! ... Dak!" I caught his arm.

"I don't want you here! There's no other way I can say it!"

"Dak, where is he?"

"Who? What do you mean?"

"You know! Jim. Where is he?"

"I don't know!" He almost spit it out. He might as well have struck me.

"Dak!"

"I'm sorry, Reena ... Look, if I tell you something of him, will you leave? Go from this place tonight?"

"All right," I said, only in desperation.

"Come back in here," he said, drawing me into the little room again.

"Dak, I don't understand."

"I don't want you to understand! You are out of it!"

"I'm not! I'm here! Tell me!"

"He's alive."

"Oh, God ..."

"I saw him about seven years ago in a hospital in London. In fact, I took him there ... as I had promised."

His words rang true, but something in his eyes warned me to be careful.

"And?"

"And I lost track of him. I returned to Africa. We didn't write ... You must know ..."

"About what?"

"About the Massacre," he said darkly.

"No. Where I have been, there was no news."

"I could not tell you, Reena." He sighed. "It would take forever. And I have so little time."

He glanced at his watch desperately. Then he softened for just a moment and held my face in his hands. "Oh, Reena, I loved you once. But I tried like hell to get over it, and I think I did. And now you are back in my life, and I am touching you ... but that doesn't make any difference. Too much has happened to everyone, everywhere! You don't belong here. Go home to your place of peace and forget me ... forget him! We are not worthy of your love anymore."

Go home to your place of peace ... how could he know of La Casa de la Paz?

"Dak, what has happened? What, at least, has happened to you?"

"It is what has not happened yet. When that is finished, I will be free."

And this time he was gone, and I could not follow him. The crowd had grown, packed itself together, murmured in a swarm, until the figure of a man appeared. Hahlos's plane had landed, and the bulky, unsmiling colonel was puffing along the ramp to the waiting people. He waved at a few of the eager ones and ignored others, especially the reporters. He seemed to be scanning the faces for a particular set of features. I gained the front line. I could have touched him. He felt my stare challenging him and answered it with a frightening look, one that revealed his own fear, his own knowledge of what was to come. He knew who I was, I'm sure of it. Perhaps not my name, but my face, and he was about to speak to me. He had bent slightly in my direction, and that is what saved his life, for at that moment, a muffled shot split the crowd and sent them rolling back, leaving Colonel Edmunde Hahlos with a hole in his neck instead of his heart.

And then I understood. I didn't want to. I fought it, with all of my sanity, with all of my will, but I knew. I knew whose hand had held that gun!

Everything blurred together after that—the big man falling at my feet, the police closing in and then spreading out in search of the assassin, forcing the people back with their batons.

"Look out, miss, you're going to get hurt!" one of them said to me brusquely.

The ambulance, the stretcher, the siren, the screaming crowd all became one mass of confusion and noise, and I fled. I fled to my quiet room on the back side of the street, overlooking a picturesque, miniature park with a well-tended, green lawn and freshly clipped shrubs and laughing, carefree children, black ... and white.

✛ ✛ ✛

I bought the newspaper only to see if Hahlos was still alive. The headlines announced at every street corner, "Colonel Sniped! Assassin at Large! Hahlos Clings to Life!" I didn't care about anything else, and I guess I really didn't care about Colonel Hahlos. My heart escaped with his dark enemy down some lonely alley to a hidden room in a hidden burrow of the teeming city.

Oh, Dak, how could you have come to this? Then something caught my eye, just one word in large print on the last page of the crumbled newspaper: *Peacetime* ... I read on, anxiously ... *Peacetime Publications, now hiring, students, housewives, world travelers, anyone with experiences to share and a willingness to work ...*

I read no further. My heart throbbed. Peacetime Publications ... La Casa de la Paz ... Dar es Salaam! A connection in name only, but still ... I would go there in the morning. If there was no job for me, I would return to the peaceful hills of New Mexico.

Dak ... I cannot help you now. Whatever you want to happen, I cannot be a part of it. But I must stay one more day, one more hour, to learn if I have a destiny in this place.

✛   ✛   ✛

Dawn again, hazy, windless, light without light on shadows that were not shadows, just the remnants of sleep, and I rose with the same hope that had let me rest in this unfamiliar place. I dressed slowly and went downstairs to an all-night café and studied the phone book. "Peacetime Publications is devoted to making public works of literature that through their words attempt to promote peace or by their example show the need for peace throughout the world ..." It said a lot more in its full-page ad, but that was enough for me. And the building was ten blocks and two hours away.

At nine o'clock, I stood before the personnel manager full of anticipation but having a difficult time explaining myself to the woman whose name plate read Mrs. Marian Harris.

"I ... I just wondered if you might have a job for me."

"What can you do? Type?"

"Not well."

"File?"

"I suppose ..."

"Make coffee?"

"What? As a matter of fact, no."

"I'm joking, of course, but still wondering exactly why you came to us."

I sat down, my enthusiasm wavering.

"I don't know, Mrs. Harris ... I saw the ad in the paper ..."

"We have many ads, young lady."

"The one that begins, 'Now hiring students ...' I have it right here." I handed her the clipping.

"Oh, that one ... yes, well, which of those are you?"

"None ... but I have been in Africa."

Her eyes brightened.

"As a missionary for four years," I added.

She sighed.

"And I just left a school for orphans in New Mexico. Its name was La Casa de la Paz."

She didn't react to the coincidence of the name.

"How long were you there?" she asked.

"Nearly seven years."

"And you haven't been anywhere else?"

"No ..."

"Or read anything published by this company?"

"No, I haven't. I'm sorry."

"Have you ever heard of *Memoirs on an African Morning*?"

"Why no, but it sounds like something I would read."

"You should have read it already."

"I was rather isolated."

"That's just my point, uh, Miss Pavane. You are far too—shall we say—naïve about the world situation. Your experience, I daresay, seems so ... limited. Have you ever even been in New York?"

"No," I answered sadly, and then I clutched at a straw. "I was at the airport last night."

She leaned forward with more interest.

"You were?"

"I could have touched Colonel Hahlos when he collapsed!"

"Well, this may be something. I'm not sure they are working on that yet. But you are a bright young woman and sincere. Go down to the assistant manager's office. It's at the end of the hall there, to the right. He may be able to use you."

I was hurrying out when she called me back.

"By the way, she said, he is the author of *Memoirs*. If I were you, I wouldn't want to ignore that."

And she smiled.

"Thank you, Mrs. Harris … I'll remember."

I rushed down the hallway, into life again, and I was not prepared for the first step! All I had to do was open that door, that door behind which was someone who could give me new purpose, but my hand faltered on the knob, and my head fell soundlessly against the gold lettering on the glass.

The man's name was printed there. It said: Jim Stone.

All the darkness of my world fell away. I couldn't believe it, but I did believe it. Of course. Who else would write *Memoirs on an African Morning*. It was his language, the way he liked alliteration in his titles, the use of light as a symbol. *Oh God, just open the door!*

There was a slender, plain-faced woman in the center of the spacious outer office, and she looked up when I came in, with a warm smile that made her seem pretty. I could hardly speak.

"Yes? May I help you?"

"I want to see Jim. I mean Mr. Stone."

"Would you like to make an appointment?"

"An appointment?" I whispered. "After eight years?"

"What? Speak up, dear."

She began thumbing busily through a thick green notebook, but at that moment, the intercom clicked on, and his voice filled the room with its warmth and its depth, and then I knew it was real.

"Liv? I'm going out in a few minutes, and I won't be back until three. Can you hold off the calls on this Hahlos thing?"

"Yes, sir."

"And that includes any hotshot news reporters. I know how they get inside information. I was once one myself!"

The sound of his voice overwhelmed me. I leaned against his secretary's desk, and she seemed not to know what to do with me.

"Did you want an appointment?"

"I just want to sit down."

"Of course …"

I barely made it to the bench by the door. Everything was whirling around me. When he entered the room, I could not see him through my tears. And I did not realize it then, but the shock of my presence was far greater to him than his was to me. At least Dak had told me he was alive. He asked Liv softly, "Who is that girl?"

She hesitated. "She hasn't mentioned her name."

I put my head down, feeling faint, and he came over to me.

"What's wrong, young lady? Are you all right?"

He was so close … so close. I just looked up and said his name. "Jim …"

For a breathless moment, he froze. Then he was pulling me to my feet and crushing me against his chest and burying his head in my hair.

He cried, "Oh my God, Reena! Reena!"

Liv had discreetly left the room at the sight of my face when I said Jim's name, and so I let my arms encircle him and draw him even closer, and I thought I would die, so great was my joy. It was forever before he could say anything, but finally, with his head pressed against mine, he whispered, "Reena … how I have loved you all these years, even believing you had died. Thank God, thank God, it wasn't true."

"Oh, Jim …"

"Let me look at you," he said, kissing my cheek and then my mouth with so much gentleness and so much longing that I could not let go.

"Ah, Reena, you're here, but there is so little time."

I shook my head. The nightmare was coming back.

"Why do you say that, Jim? About time? Dak said it too, those exact words."

"Don't say his name to me!"

"What is it, Jim? What is happening? I'm afraid …"

"And well you should be, my love," he said softly, "but I have no answer to the riddle. Perhaps you do. Dak told me you were dead!"

"Oh no! Listen, Jim, he told me, just last night, that he hadn't seen you for seven years. That isn't true, is it?"

"God, no, he's been in New York over a year. It seems that he wants to keep us apart," he said bitterly. "Oh, Reena, let's not talk about him. Let's talk about us."

"I have loved you since that first night in your hallway, when my world was crashing in around me, and you made a place for me in your heart. I didn't know how to tell you …" I began.

He cut off my words with a kiss, and I was standing in that hall again.

"When Dak said you were dead, I didn't quite believe it. The story just didn't completely convince me."

"What story?"

"Dak sent me a photograph from Africa of a girl killed in a plane crash. It could have been you. There was no name, but the young lady had been on her way to England. Dak was sure you would have gone there, if you left Africa, knowing it was my home. I had to believe it. But it almost killed me."

"If only I hadn't given up. If only I had tried to find you," I could barely say.

"But you did find me. Now is all that matters," he said, hugging me again. His heart was pounding against my ear. We sat down on the hardwood bench, his hands clutching mine as if I were a lifeline for his long-drifting heart.

"But why are you here? In New York?"

"I was following Colonel Hahlos. He refused to tell me anything about you when I found him in Dar es Salaam. And a few days ago, he was in New Mexico on his speaking tour. When I heard him say he was going to New York, I got on a plane that night. I came here … looking for a job, something to do until I could figure things out. When I saw your name on the door, I forgot about everything else. Oh, Jim, there's so much I don't know!"

"In time, Reena, in time …"

"You said there was not much time."

"Yes."

"What did you mean?"

"I'm not sure ... After Hahlos was shot last night, I had a strange premonition. I can't quite make sense out of it."

"I can."

"You ... can?"

"Dak fired that shot, Jim."

"What?"

"I saw him, talked to him, just moments before! He was jumpy and tense, and he would hardly look at me. He kept telling me it was no place for me and that I would soon understand why, as if he knew what was going to happen."

"But knowing about it and doing it are two different things."

"You still defend him, don't you?"

"He saved my life."

"Then why did he lie to you ... and make these veiled threats?"

"That's what's nagging at me."

"He wanted me to go back to New Mexico ... without seeing you. He wants you, alone."

"It looks that way, doesn't it? But I want to trust him. Need to really. Otherwise I'd be afraid of every shadow."

"I thought you would be friends."

"We were, Reena. The best. We just didn't see things, the things that happened in Africa, the same way. It couldn't be helped. I tried, and I think he did, too. There was no bridging the gap."

"Of color?"

"No, never that. At least, not for me. He became very enamored of King Kisasi's blacks, their heritage, their dreams. I don't know. He began to change in that Vitani camp. He even told me years ago, on the way out of the jungle, not to trust him."

"He was a Christian!"

"Then I ... shall never be," Jim said.

"I sent a boy back to him, a boy who wanted to believe!"

"I remember ... one of your guards."

"Yes."

"He came to us. But Dak frightened him away with riddles and sarcasm. The boy was confused. He knew there was something more to the story. I wished then with all my heart I could have helped him."

"Is that in your book?"

"*Memoirs*?"

I nodded.

"Yes, it is."

"I haven't read it, Jim, but I feel as if I know its essence."

"You are a part of it, though I never use your name."

"I've been sheltered ... from everything, for so many years. Hold on to me, Jim. I don't want to go back, not ever."

"What is it that you left behind?"

"A little peace ... a little loneliness ... a lot of love ... I've been teaching at an orphanage near Taos for seven years."

"The desert was good to you. It might be better ... if you did go back."

"Not for me. But I'll do whatever you ask."

He gazed at me with compassion and said, "Be my love ..."

The door opened, and Liv strode in businesslike and composed. My presence must have an explanation. Jim dropped his arms and introduced us. "Miss Pavane, this is my personal secretary, Liv Collier. Liv, this is Reena Pavane."

She looked at me with something brightening in her eyes and said, "I think I know who you are. It is a great pleasure to meet you, and I am glad to know your name at last. Call me Liv."

Jim smiled a quick thank-you to her and led me out into the hall. He could hardly keep from touching me and looking into my eyes, but it was the last place he could let his feelings show.

"There's someone I want you to meet ... for an assignment, if you're willing."

"Of course."

People stared at us curiously. Jim did not seem to notice them, even when they spoke to him, and I was still wiping away tears when a door opened suddenly on our left, and a striking, well-tailored woman with glossy, black hair stood there transfixed.

"Jim, what is the meaning of this?"

"It seems that Personnel has refused this young lady a job—no experience, no formal education," Jim answered.

"How ridiculous!" the woman said righteously. "How is one supposed to learn? Show her to the ladies' room, Jim. She can wash her face and come back to my office. But she must hurry. I have several appointments today …"

And she disappeared behind the cold, gray door, a glimpse of radiance gone.

"Jim, who is she?" I asked, but something about her stature, her way of speaking to Jim instead of to me, her familiar tone when she used his name, told me who she was before he said, "My wife."

"Oh … I should have known … She's very beautiful."

"Yes, she is."

"Does she love you?"

He glanced at me with that teasing half-smile that I remembered so well.

"We … get along."

"That's not what I asked you."

He sighed. "In her own way, I guess. She didn't leave me when I was sick. She stuck it out. And I was in pretty bad shape, physically and emotionally. But she stood by while I worked it out. She never complained. And so, I didn't leave her when I was well again … Here we are, love. I'll wait for you."

We still had not touched again, and now he said, "You know … I will leave her now."

"Jim, don't talk of it yet."

"I love you, Reena. Nothing can change that."

"I know," I said, breaking down again and rushing from the sight of his dear face.

The cool water felt good on my burning cheeks, but I only wanted to go back to him, to feel his arm on mine, to hear his voice, dusky and warm, to stand in his shadow, if that's all of him I could ever have. *Oh God, we are together again. What more could I ask?* And then I had a sobering thought. *Dakimu!* Would he always be there between us, the key to life and death, as he surely had been in the past? And what must we do, now that the three of us are together again, and Colonel Hahlos? The mark had done its job well. I looked at my arm where I'd rolled up the sleeve. The cross gleamed up at me, and I traced its outline with my finger. *You are not through with us, yet, are you, Lord? We still have crosses to bear, God help us.* And I went back to Jim.

This time he put his arms around me right there in the corridor.

"Jim …"

"I don't care, let them see. I love you more than my own life. What does reputation matter? Even Nadine must know sooner or later."

"How can I work for her?"

My voice was muffled, my face hidden in his shoulder.

"You won't mind, you'll see. She's very professional—never personal, never emotional. She is organized and polite but never passionate."

We were standing at her door.

"Where are you staying?"

I told him quickly.

"I'll call you later."

"Okay … Am I all right?"

"You look fine, my beautiful girl."

He touched my cheek with a light hand, his eyes filling with tears.

"Smile now," he said and had to turn away.

✝   ✝   ✝

Nadine Stone greeted me with the same cool voice that she had used with Jim.

"Well now, that's better. What's your name, young lady?"

"Reena Pavane."

"Age?"

"Twenty-eight."

"Place of birth?"

"Forest Home, California."

"Schools? Colleges?"

"All in Forest Home, Mrs. Stone. But when I was sixteen and a junior in high school, my parents went on a mission to Africa, and they took me with them."

"Oh … I see. A mission."

"To Christianize a small village of natives." I paused. *I can't tell her where. Surely the name Huzuni is in Jim's book.* "In northern Africa," I finished.

"Were you successful?"

"Somewhat."

"I am interested in Africa, of course, because of Jim's experiences there. You've read his *Memoirs*?"

"No, but I intend to."

"Good, here's a copy. Read it tonight."

I thought I'd be in Jim's arms that night and agonized over being so callous with Nadine's heart and my sense that it wasn't right. I loved him so much I could barely breathe glancing at his picture on Nadine's desk, probably taken during those years we were separated from what we had felt for each other in Africa. He looked so vulnerable and sad, still thin from the illness that had driven him from Tanzania. In that photo he thought I was dead. Now I could make everything right. But what that was, I didn't know yet.

"Reena, are you listening?" Nadine broke into my imagining.

"Yes," I said.

She handed me a large, handsomely bound volume with the title stamped in gold letters and continued, "You especially need to pay attention to the parts where Jim is with a native he calls the Black. I think that man is lurking around here in New York, up to no good."

That black, my dear Dakimu, who took me to Jim probably right on those pages!

"I'll be anxious to read the book, Mrs. Stone."

"I daresay it will move you deeply, since you have some ties with the country," she said.

"I'm sure it will."

"Fine. Now there's a possible story involving Africa that Jim and I are considering. You could perhaps help us, but I'm not prepared to give you any details yet. Shall we begin by having you file some research material?"

"That would be fine, Mrs. Stone."

"All right ... Oh, where did you go after Africa? Surely you have not been there all this time."

"No, I came home and went on my own mission to New Mexico. I worked among the Indians and—"

"That's enough. More of the same thing I take it, Christianizing?"

"Yes, and teaching."

"The Bible?"

"Yes, and some English skills. Many of the children only spoke Spanish."

"Yes, well, that's all very good, Miss Pavane, but are you able to deal with the world you are now in?"

"I am here."

"The story we may do concerns the very black man I was mentioning." She sighed. "I might as well tell you his name. Dakimu Reiman. I'm sure he's never had the benefit of your teaching. He's as savage as they come! Do you think you could interview a man like that?"

I stared at her. There was a cry in my throat. *No! Never! Not to hurt him!* I answered silently.

But I said, almost choking on the words, "Yes, I think ... I could do that. I'm not afraid of him."

"Do you know him?" she asked, incredulous.

"I know who he is, that's all."

"You've seen pictures?"

"Yes."

"A handsome man ..."

"Yes."

"But a devil!" she said bitterly.

"Do *you* know him?"

"More than I'd like to," she answered quickly.

"Is there anything else you want to know about me, Mrs. Stone?"

"No, not today. You have your book to read. Come back tomorrow, same time."

"I'll be here … and thank you for giving me a chance."

"Oh, don't thank me. Thank Jim."

"I … will."

I could not get out of there fast enough. I was never good at lying. What would it do to her if she knew how close I had been to Jim and to Dak? I went to Jim's office. Liv Collier greeted me with a relaxed smile.

"Oh, Miss Pavane, hello again. Mr. Stone left you a note. He was late for a meeting."

And she handed me a small, sealed envelope. I didn't read it until I reached the deserted park beneath my window. There I sat on the grass and gazed at his handwriting and realized I had never seen it before. It said, *I love you … Keep smiling … Until six … Jim.*

I went inside and opened *Memoirs on an African Morning* and felt a shock when I read the first words. Even though I had lived it, those desperate days with Dak, the crossing of the flooded river, meeting Hahlos on the road with his Vitani guardians, my hour with Jim, finding the chloroquine that restored him for what else he would have to endure, Dak's promise to bring him back, I could not believe how clearly he had painted the agony of those days. He made it seem that the land itself had suffered in our passing.

For eight years, I feared he was dead, and here was the story, without my name, without Dak's name. He had protected us, while exposing many others, both black and white. It seemed a supreme act of loyalty. Readers always wanted names, if not to validate the events, then to satisfy their curiosity. Nadine would finally figure out who I was. Ironic that she handed me the book as required reading for a job at Peacetime!

Jim's words were full of passion for Africa, even the parts about his imprisonment. He had made friends among the Vitani, let the children take pictures with his camera, taught them some English—the word *peace*, the word *love.* He seemed so grateful to be alive that he wrote without judgment. He gave both sides equal space. He showed no anger toward his captors but much remorse for his countrymen's shaping of the conflict, much poetic language about the African landscape, its rivers and valleys, sunsets and storms.

But what had the most profound effect on me were the photographs. How he got them I couldn't imagine, and how he escaped with them was an even greater mystery. There were shots of children playing like any other children, but on closer examination, you could see the fierceness, the hunger for conflict in their eyes. One boy had gouged out the eye of another over a broken spear! This picture was one of a group of prints entitled *The Means to an End?* The last photo in that section was by far the most damaging, but then, if you went back, you saw it in the very first one, in the face of the angry child.

This last showed warriors returning from battle, killing their wounded and dying with spears in hearts, vines around throats, so they could enter the village singing and whole, the missing men heroes, never burdens or bringers of blood into the tidy, unstained streets where the celebrations began.

How could Dak have known about this and still become one of them? There were no photos of Dakimu or of me. There was Nathan beneath the helicopter. He had taken that one, after all. There was Hahlos being readied to leave the camp with his black battalion. Oh so many. It was a complete and irrevocable tale. He even blamed himself at the end ...

> *I decry the violence, I abhor the pain, damn the deceitfulness of men, black or white, who maneuver lives like pawns, leaving the victims no choice, how they shall live, how they shall die.*
>
> *I saw the black deception, I saw the white deception (here the pictures of rifles from France and the United States), I saw good men become monsters, I saw monsters become murderers.*
>
> *Ah, Africa, it is not only you. We are all to blame. It is not the country, it is not the color; it is the hearts of men who betray, when they cannot love enough. Even I betrayed to bring this story to the world, and I shall pay. My morning song shall be my* kwa heri.
>
> *But I shall be ready. I shall not slip away. And I leave you with this: if any suffer because of my words, whether justly or unjustly, whether*

they are the monsters or the victims, then that is my punishment. You can do me no further harm.

When I am gone, the truth shall still abide. Though the hatred remains, the ruin rages, the color clashes in the dark of night, there comes again the dawn, when the morning sun blesses with light my African home.

The phone rang sharply, lifting me out of my memories of that powerful time, living life for life itself.

"Hello, my angel."

"Oh, Jim, it's beautiful, so beautiful …"

"What is, love?"

"Your book."

"Nadine gave you a copy?"

"Required reading."

He laughed and said, "Wouldn't you like an autographed copy?"

"As a matter of fact …"

"I'll be right there!"

"Don't you have to go home?"

"I do, yes, tonight anyway. We're meeting with the manager of Peacetime about our new book."

"The one about Dak."

It was a statement, not a question, and he was surprised.

"Nadine told you?"

"Yes."

"What do you think?"

"I don't know. I know I can't work on it."

"She'll want you to."

"What shall I tell her?"

"What did you tell her already?"

"Nothing … I mean, I lied to her, Jim. I said I'd been in North Africa all those years. I couldn't tell her anything that might tie us together."

"I'm glad you didn't, although you'd be surprised how fast she could have East Africa within walking distance of North Africa! Reena, I just decided you're coming with me to this dinner meeting. We'll pick you up in twenty minutes."

"But, Jim …"

"Bye, love," he said softly, hanging up.

How can I face seeing them together?

I changed my clothes, wondering if my definitely New Mexican attire was appropriate. The long sleeves, of course, would hide the mark that Nadine knew was on Jim's arm. All of us in the same city now, Hahlos and Dakimu at odds with each other, and Jim and I at odds with them. Who was writing this story?

☩   ☩   ☩

It started out as a pleasant evening. I liked the manager of Peacetime Publications immediately. He was outspoken and good-natured. He didn't drink, although Jim and Nadine kept offering him some of the bottle they kept filling their glasses with.

Once Jim said, "You know, Hal, I really don't like this stuff, but it takes the edge off my nerves."

"Wait till it starts in on the nerves themselves, my boy!" he quipped, and everyone laughed. He had a way of putting us at ease, which I thought, considering the situation, took some doing. His name was Harold Tarrington, and he was not a young man. His hair hung straight from the center of his head and was cut like the schoolboy whose father had set a bowl on his crown and trimmed around it with the kitchen scissors. It was dark gray and still thick and I thought rather distinguished-looking.

I never saw him frown. Even when Nadine cut him off or provoked arguments, he bounced right back with wisdom and charm. He must have done wonders for the image of Peacetime Publications. He tried to include me in the conversation, but Nadine was not happy about my presence, and she outdid him.

When he asked, "Miss Pavane, what understanding of blacks did you reach in your contact with Africans?" Nadine cried immediately, before

I could open my mouth, "Oh, what could she know, except what they thought of the story of creation!"

"I should be interested even in that, young lady," he said to me, bemused.

"I believe dinner is ready, Harold, and I absolutely refuse to talk of savages at my dinner table," she said, ignoring his comment to me.

"The furthest thing from my mind, Nadine, I assure you," he bantered, with an ironic grin, since, after all, we were there to talk about the best of them, Dakimu Reiman, but she missed it, and Jim squeezed my hand behind her back.

✢ ✢ ✢

The dinner was excellent, although Nadine had not cooked it, but Jim and I were terribly uneasy. Hal Tarrington sensed this and made an admirable effort to keep the conversation light. But everyone was thinking of afterward and the discussion of the mysterious black from Africa, and that would be a tense conversation by any standards. Mr. Tarrington was especially attentive to me, and Nadine gave him quizzical looks throughout the meal. He kept his word and did not talk about blacks, but he got me to tell him something about La Casa de la Paz and the orphaned Indians and Mexican Americans and how the name of my home in New Mexico had led me to Jim's door. Nadine was completely bored and kept fidgeting for Hal's attention.

Finally, she broke in, "Oh, all this talk of orphans! It's so depressing, and why on earth was the place called the House of Peace? The state of those children sounds perfectly miserable."

"But there was peace there, Mrs. Stone, because they were loved," I said defensively.

"Of course, you told them God loved them," she said, as if that were an answer.

"No ... First, we loved them. If we had not loved them, they could never have understood God's love," I replied quietly.

"Oh, all this 'love' business. Isn't it enough for peace to mean 'not hating'? Do we have to go around loving every poor wretch?"

"I think we do," I answered calmly.

"And so do I, Nadine," their friend said firmly. "On this idea, I believe you are outnumbered. Jim?"

"Yes, Hal … I have to agree. It isn't enough not to hate. You must believe in love, if you can't always give it yourself. It's a hard thing, peace. It takes more than tolerance, more than indifference. It takes … love. There is no other way to say it, and it's not easy to say. Some people … are not easy to love."

"Well, I think we have thoroughly discussed this subject," Nadine informed us and rose without looking at anyone, mumbling something about "tending to the dessert myself."

She missed the look that Jim and I exchanged but not the moment Hal put his hand over mine on the starched, white linen tablecloth. No one said anything while we ate our thinly iced, little cakes and drank our coffee. I only wished it were all over.

On the way to the living room a few minutes later, I overheard Nadine say to Jim, "She's a bit young for him, don't you think?"

"How do you know I brought her along for him, my dear?" he said, and she fumed but smiled sweetly.

"Why, Jim, you've only just met her!"

"Then you will excuse me while I get to know her better," he said to her, and then to me, "Miss Pavane, won't you come with me for a breath of fresh air?"

We went out onto a wide terrace, where he stood apart from me, staring out into the black, moonless night. "I had to get out of there," he said, shaking his head as if fighting off a bad dream, and then, "This is harder than I thought it would be … having you here."

"We'll be all right, Jim. Just tell me what's going on, what happened today?"

"I spoke to Dakimu," he said softly.

"What?"

"He called right in the middle of an argument with Nadine, an argument about you, actually."

He moved a little closer to me.

"Nadine was going on and on about how you were a missionary and what possible use could you be, too innocent, too scared. She was reconsidering giving you the interview with Dak, because surely you hadn't been allowed to get too close to the blacks."

I thought of the river bank and my arms around Dak and his wanting to kiss me.

Jim went on, "She said you wouldn't know what to do with a Dakimu Reiman. And then he called."

I waited while the story spilled out. Nadine had walked out abruptly when the phone rang. Jim said he was angry at first, so angry that Dak had told him I was dead. He told him how I had shown up at his office that very day. Dak was defensive, saying how everything fit, the time, the place, everything about the plane crash, that he was startled when he saw me at the airport. He said he was sorry, but that wasn't why he called.

Jim's voice was hoarse now. He spoke as if trying to expel the ghosts of a thousand years. "Dak said we had a score to settle, that we had better not publish any more reports about him. I said we would not implicate him in the Hahlos thing, but he didn't believe me, kept ranting about *Memoirs*, how people would recognize him, accuse him of crimes. Maybe someone had seen him with you and that could further damage him."

"He won't hurt me," I broke in.

"Then why did he lie to me and ignore you himself all these years? He could have found you. Unless he thought you had given up waiting for him to keep his promise. Given up and disappeared, and he thought the plane crash might have been true after all. The picture in the news clipping did look like you, Reena. I just fell apart. Nadine thought it was the malaria, but it was losing you, losing you before we had really found each other."

"Better now than never," I whispered, touching his arm where the cross simmered. "We can't know what Dak was thinking. We have to let it go, Jim."

"Here we are hating Dakimu's lie, while we're lying to Nadine and the rest of the world that wants a piece of him!" He hesitated, and then asked, "Can you stand to uphold that lie? Can you even stand her?"

"I can do more than that. I can love her."

"It won't do you any good. I've tried, I really have."

"I know. She is senseless to waste your love."

He caressed my hand for a moment and said, "If I believed in God, I would be on my knees, thanking Him for you."

✛   ✛   ✛

We returned reluctantly to the dining room. Nadine and Hal Tarrington were in a heated discussion, her voice elevated in irritation, but Hal was saying, "If you tell this story, Nadine, you'll tell it straight or not at all!"

"But it's a good angle, a sensational one!" she argued vehemently.

"We are not after the sensational, Nadine, only the human, the actual—"

"What is so sensational?" Jim asked, coming behind me into the room.

"Oh, Jim, listen, Hal can be so stubborn sometimes! I just had a call from Sonya Ferrans—you remember her, the woman with that silly Pekinese you detest? Anyway, her oldest daughter, Susan, is out at USC, and on the spur of the moment, she decided to come home for a week, no classes or something, and you'll never guess, by a fantastic coincidence she was given a last-minute seat on Colonel Hahlos's plane! She sat three seats from him, in fact. And that's not all! In that confusion at the airport, keeping her eyes alert only for Susie, who should she see, almost knocked her down, Dak Reiman! He was quite flustered, she said, and skittered away nervously, looking back over his shoulder several times. Of course, she doesn't know the man, only who he is, but she said the whole thing was funny, you know, just odd, and Sonya has a sixth sense about human nature—"

Jim stopped her before she could go on. "I wouldn't give that woman six cents for what she knows about anything!"

"Oh, Jim, you're so negative. What do you think, Miss Pavane?" she asked, gazing above our heads, as if seeing the book jacket blurb there ... "'Black man from Africa greets white expert on African affairs at Kennedy Airport, as friend or foe?' How does that sound? Or maybe, 'To befriend or to blast?' That's it, that's better. I like the implication."

"I think it's wrong."

"What? What's that, Miss Pavane?" Nadine asked, amazed at my audacity.

But I went on. "To implicate a man in a charge as serious as ... murder, whether or not the authorities had questioned him or even suspected him."

"I wholeheartedly agree, Miss Pavane, and quite respect your answer," Mr. Tarrington said and then turned to Nadine, "Now let's hold off on the accusations and see what we do have."

She grumbled her acquiescence, and he continued soberly, "Simply the journey of a black born, raised, and educated in Africa to the United States in a controversial time of black studies, black civil liberties, black social integration. We want his background, his opinions, his purpose for being in this country."

"And what if that black man doesn't wish that journey to be public information?" Jim said.

"All the more reason to do it!" Nadine said forcefully. "He must be hiding something!"

"We do not expose people in that way, Nadine. I shouldn't have to remind you," said the manager of Peacetime Publications.

"We exposed a lot of people in Jim's *Memoirs!*" she reminded us.

"Those things were based on fact, not on supposition."

"But if the exposure aids the cause of peace ..." Nadine said, not backing down.

"I don't see how it can. We must not distort this black man's intentions, whatever they are. I will do nothing without an interview. If he objects to that, we close the book. Surely you can see the position we are in."

"Of course, Hal," Jim said. "But I would like to try to get that interview."

"Yes, I think the story is worth a try. But we must leave out any suspicions about his presence at the airport."

"But that's the best part!" Nadine cried.

"Only to a vengeful mind, my girl." Tarrington sighed. "I hope you will excuse me, I'm rather tired. It was a lovely dinner, Nadine. I hope I shall be invited back."

"Of course, dear," she said sweetly. "This fencing is all part of the game. I don't take it personally."

"I'm glad ... Jim?" He grasped his hand warmly. "I'm sorry to leave you just now. We'll talk in the morning."

"Won't you at least stay for more coffee?" Mrs. Stone pressured.

"No ... thank you, Nadine. I've had enough ... of everything."

He was turning to me, saying, "Miss Pavane, the pleasure was all mine. I hope we shall become friends."

"That would be wonderful," I said.

He smiled. "Keep up the good work!"

"I have made my share of mistakes," I said.

"Ah, but how many times have you done the right thing?"

"Not enough ... God knows, not enough," I answered painfully, remembering Huzuni and Dakimu and the cold, hateful eyes of King Kisasi.

"But your life is still so new, my young friend. You have many years yet ... to love," he said gently.

Nadine was cutting in again, "Oh, Hal, would you be a dear and take Reena back to her hotel?"

"Of course, if she wishes."

"That would be nice. I'm tired, too."

Nadine disappeared to find my sweater, and Hal to start his car, and Jim reached for my hands.

"Thanks for being here," he said.

"Jim ... I'm not going to say good-bye."

"I know. Until tomorrow?"

"Tomorrow."

✛   ✛   ✛

I felt safe with Hal Tarrington. We rode in an easy silence for a few miles, and then he said, "Don't let Mrs. Stone upset you, Reena. She can break your heart."

"No ... it won't be her," I said, shaking my head.

"Do you know who it will be?"

"Yes."

"May I know?" he asked compassionately.

"Why?"

"Perhaps I can protect you."

"You are very kind, but this is something we must face alone."

"We?"

"Jim and I."

"Miss Pavane, you are a mystery to me. But I know Jim. I know what he fears and why."

"We have the same fears."

"I am an old man, Reena, and I have made mistakes, too. Perhaps I can rectify a few of them by helping you."

"There is no help for us," I whispered.

"I don't understand something. You and Jim, did you not only just meet today?"

"No … it was a long time ago. I'll show you what I have shown to no one for almost eight years."

And I rolled my sleeve back from the mark on my arm and thrust the ragged scar of the cross beneath his eyes.

"Oh my God! Like Jim's! Just like Jim's."

"Yes, sir."

"How could that be?"

"We were both held captive by King Kisasi in Africa and branded with this mark."

"Does Nadine know?"

"No."

"Does anyone?"

"Yes … there are two others who have the same mark, and they are both in this city."

"What!"

He had stopped the car when I first revealed my terrible mark, and now he waited, visibly shaken.

I went on, "The bearers of this tortured cross are men in pain still and bitter conflict. Can you guess?"

"I guess at one," he said. "Dakimu?"

"Yes ..."

"And the other?"

"Colonel Edmunde Hahlos."

He stared at me amazed.

"I don't begin to understand the meaning of all this, Reena," he said sorrowfully, "but I'm glad you told me. Just remember, you have an ally in me."

"I knew that, Mr. Tarrington, when we met."

He smiled, with some concern still on his face. "I'm very fond of Jim, you know, and he's been under tremendous pressure lately. After *Memoirs* was published last year, the critics came out of the woodwork. For a while, all he got were recriminations. 'Why wasn't this information released sooner? Why didn't you come forward before the Massacre? You could have saved thousands of lives!' was the general outcry. In the first place, he was emotionally drained for a long time. He told me once that for months he felt he had nothing to live for and nothing to die for."

He hesitated and then went on, "You probably know this, although I'm sure Nadine doesn't ... A woman he had loved in Africa was tragically killed in a plane crash, and it just sapped the last of his strength. Then his black friend, who had brought him safely through the warring tribes and back to England, left him to return to Africa, and he was lost."

"Mr. Tarrington," I whispered, "I am that woman."

"But how ...?"

"Jim's black friend told him I was dead. The rest is not hard to figure out, but I'll tell you. That black friend was Dakimu Reiman!"

"Oh, my child ... my poor children!" he cried, taking my hand like a father. "What can I do?"

"You have listened. That is a lot."

We had started moving again when he said, "It would please me if you would call me Hal, Reena."

"Well ... Hal ... I think I will sleep tonight. For one night, at least, this city will seem a little less forbidding ... It's in the next block."

He slowed down.

"Reena, may I ask you something else about Dakimu?"

"Of course, but I don't know if I can answer. He is changed …"

"I think you will know." He paused, as if choosing his words carefully, but what he asked was simply, "Was the black in love with you, too?"

"Yes."

"Ah, it becomes clearer, this jigsaw picture."

"I wish it were as clear to me. I wish I knew why I had to be kept apart from Jim for eight years! I wish I knew why Dak did not keep his promise, if he loved me."

"What was that?"

"Not only to bring Jim out of Kisasi's camp alive, but to bring him back to me! He could have found me, Hal. I did not disappear. And if I have figured it out right, I had only just left Dar es Salaam. It wouldn't have been difficult to follow me … There is a missing piece, and I must find it. I must find it before Jim does!"

We were in front of the hotel.

"Don't get out, Hal. I'll be all right."

"Nonsense!" he teased. "I always see a lady to her door!"

And in a moment, we were climbing the softly carpeted stairway and speaking of trivialities, the tension gone, when we came face to face with a hunched, shadowy form and the black, unsmiling countenance of Dakimu Reiman.

Black

When I heard them coming, I thought to turn the corner and hide in another doorway, but why should I be afraid? I had loved them, and they had loved me. It would be a happy scene. But I did not count on her being with someone besides Jim. When I saw who it was, it was too late. So I stepped forward to meet them and held out my hand.

"Mr. Tarrington, I don't think I've had the pleasure …"

"Mr. Reiman, I must say this is a strange place for our first encounter."

"And yet not so strange," I said quietly. "She is a new friend of yours … and an old friend of mine."

"What do you want?" Hal said roughly.

"To speak to my old friend, Reena Pavane."

Tarrington hesitated, but she said, "Hal, it's all right. I want to talk to him. He will not hurt me."

And I loved her so standing in the shadows. It all came back to me … her hand in mine on the banks of the Rufiji, her arms around me in the raging flood and again by the peaceful pool, her heart crying out to me over the heads of the savage blacks, "Bring him back to me," her eyes at our meeting at the airport, full of questions and forgiveness. She cleansed me, and in that moment, I could have betrayed my own cause. I was ready to give up everything to renew that tie we once had, that oneness in Christ, that union of black and white through love. I wanted it so badly. I craved it more than anything.

But her love for Jim was a monstrous wall through which I could never pass. It was a thing undeniable and beautiful, a thing I could never have, and my resolve returned.

"Do you want me to stay, Reena?" Mr. Tarrington was saying.

"No ... unless you have something to say to each other." She looked at both of us.

"Not yet," Tarrington said, "but I will be looking for you soon, Reiman."

"And I will be ready for you," I assured him.

He glanced at Reena and moved reluctantly toward the staircase.

"See you in the morning?"

"Yes ... and Hal ... thank you."

He nodded and vanished down the long, dimly lighted stairwell.

"Come in, Dak," Reena said, opening her door, and my heart raced in anguish.

I didn't want to say it, because it wasn't true, but I did. "I'm sorry, Reena, that I didn't tell you Jim was here in New York."

"I'm trying to understand it, Dak," she said. And before I could speak, she went on, "But more than that, I'm trying to understand why you didn't keep your promise."

"I did, Reena," I said, coming closer to her. "I kept him alive. I brought him out."

"But not to me!"

"You were not to be found."

"It should have been easy, Dak. Don't lie to me."

"You will hate the truth."

"All the more reason to give it to me. It is better to know the truth than to know nothing."

"Here then!"

And I handed her a scrap of paper, frayed and wrinkled and thin, that I had coveted all these years.

She stared hard at the remnant that read, where I had darkened the lines with ink, LA 3.

"Oh, Dak! Dak! Why?"

"I thought I knew then," I told her honestly. "My reasons were justified."

My hands fell upon her leather-bound, gold-leafed copy of Jim's *Memoirs*.

"Ah, yes! Here it is! Here is my justification!"

"You didn't know about that then!"

"I knew what he wanted to do! I just didn't know about the means ... the hidden cameras he carried out of that prison, the yellow notepad full of scorn!"

"There is scorn for both sides there, Dak," she said defensively.

"Don't defend him, Reena. It only makes easier what I have to do."

"Are you threatening me, Dakimu? Because I'm not afraid of you."

"Even after what you saw at the airport?"

"I saw nothing," she said, turning her head away.

"You saw Hahlos begin to recognize you and bend over slightly, just enough so that my bullet missed his heart!"

"Why do you tell me this, Dak? Haven't you done enough? Why must you wound everything you love?"

"Because I have such ... longings, unfulfilled."

"Don't we all, my friend?"

"Not like this!"

"You are no different."

"I am black!"

"I have no answer, Dak," she said helplessly. "I wish I did. I wish I could say, 'You are free. You have no debts. You have no pain.' But I have no power. There is only One who does, and you have forsaken Him."

"No! He has forsaken me!"

"'I will be with you always,' He said. Don't you believe that?"

"No. I never believed that! Your teachers could never say why we still fought and died on our own soil, struggled with disease and starvation, while the white world thrived and sent us missionaries! Missionaries, bah!"

"What did you wish them to send? Look what you did with guns."

"That was better than God!"

"Was not peace better? Peace in Christ?"

"No! He lied to us! We still suffered and killed our brothers and wept for our dying land."

"But it is man you should blame for those deeds, not God."

"I do blame man!" I cried. "I blame white man!"

She folded her hands across the *Memoirs* and studied my face.

"I still love you, Dak."

"Not as you love Jim."

"You knew that from the beginning," she said, caressing the book beneath her fingertips.

"You saved my life," I spoke the only words I was sure of, "and I saved Jim. I betrayed him, and he betrayed me. Now we are even. Now we must begin again."

"In love!"

"No, in hate!"

"There is something missing still," she said softly. "I thought I knew it all when I saw that crumpled note, where the key to our estrangement lay. But that isn't all."

Suddenly she came at me, remembering, realizing, seeking my face but tearing at the sleeve on my left arm.

"No!" I shouted.

"That's it, isn't it? It will tell me all!"

"No!"

But she was too quick for me. In an instant, my arm and my heart lay bare before her eyes. She looked down and shuddered, saying faintly, "Oh, Dak, God forgive you. God forgive you."

And she fell unconscious into my arms.

I laid her gently on her bed and covered her with a light blanket, loathing all the while the sight of my battered arm, where the mark had been hacked with fire into a thousand shameless crosses in the place of the one victorious one.

Then I opened the *Memoirs on an African Morning*, and I scribbled across the first blank page ... *What must be, must be.* I did not sign it or leave a trace of my presence there, except on her cheek, where long before she woke would dry, a tear ...

Eupe

When I woke up, the phone was screaming in my ear. I answered and heard, while my eyes absorbed Dak's words scrawled on the page before me, "It's Hal Tarrington. Get over to the office! Hahlos's IV was pulled. He may not make it this time!"

What must be ... must be.

Jim and Nadine were already there when I rushed into Hal's office. Jim looked resigned, Nadine rather subdued, and Hal Tarrington thoroughly frantic. He put his arm around me and swept me to a chair, saying secretly to me, "Thank God you're all right!"

And with my eyes, I asked him, "You haven't told Jim yet?"

"He doesn't know about Dak being at your room," he whispered and then turned to the others, pacing back and forth in front of them. They must have wondered why he had wanted me there, but Nadine recalled that I had seen Hahlos just before he was shot and decided I might be of some use.

Hal was forging ahead. "We are in a grave situation, folks. As you well know, this firm published in the name of peace some embarrassing truths about the colonel and his Council for Africa, by way of Jim's book mostly, but others have written articles for several of our magazines, analyzing his so-called 'good will' tour and finding it a farce, his speeches full of lies. According to his retinue of coworkers and friends, these publications have prejudiced the country against him and have antagonized in particular certain groups of people, blacks among them, who see Hahlos as a threat. Of course, he quite blatantly betrayed people, black and white, through the mess he and his Council made in the country he claims to know so much about, Africa. Any one of a number of them could be trying to kill him, but we are the wind that fanned the flames! In short, Hahlos's advisors demand a retraction of part or all of Jim's *Memoirs* that refer to the colonel and a public acknowledgment of his innocence in the events leading up to the Massacre."

"I won't do it, Hal!" Jim said, rising from his chair.

"Of course you won't! I wouldn't even ask you to. The man is guilty. He should suffer the consequences, public ostracism, 'Hahlos go home' signs, but murder, for Christ's sake! That is rather extreme, to put it mildly."

"May I say something?" It was Nadine.

"Yes?" Tarrington said cautiously.

"I think we should produce the assassin and get his name out in the open."

"For heaven's sake, Nadine, we aren't a detective agency!" Jim growled at her.

My heart ached. His tone frightened me.

"Sometimes you appall me," he was saying.

"The feeling is mutual, I assure you, dear," she said curtly.

"Mr. Tarrington … Hal," I interrupted. "What is the colonel's condition?"

"He's still alive, but barely. I have a man outside the door, but the incident was accomplished efficiently. There were no traces of the person who did this."

We glanced at each other, our sure knowledge bursting on the wavelengths between our eyes.

Jim broke in again. "Perhaps we should print a statement in the ten leading US newspapers deploring the use of violence, even in cases of perceived betrayal, but supporting Hahlos's right to live free from harm, making it clear we still do not support his policies."

"I like that," Hal said thoughtfully.

"I do not," Nadine countered. "It is too much of a compromise."

"That's all we can do sometimes, is compromise," Jim said in a quieter voice.

But she jumped on him, "Oh, sometimes I wonder why I married you! Don't you ever fight for anything? Your own book! You'd let them tear it to pieces, and us, too."

"You'd be surprised what I have fought for in my time," he said, and added even more calmly, "and am fighting for still."

"Well, it has nothing to do with me!" she cried angrily.

Jim leaned forward in the chair where he had sat down again and held his head in his hands. Nadine ignored him, but Hal shot me a sympathetic look and then did what I would have done. He went over to Jim, gripped his shoulders, and said, "Take it easy, Jim. This is hardest on you, I know, but we're with you. We're behind you all the way. Don't forget that."

Then he did a great thing. He turned to Nadine and asked her graciously if she would come to the press room and help him write up the statements and make calls to the newspapers. She was more than happy to go, but she questioned me on the way out.

"And what are you going to do, Miss Pavane?"

There was a hint of a sneer in it.

"I'm going to make your husband a cup of tea, Mrs. Stone," I said, not skipping a beat, and she continued through the door behind Harold Tarrington.

By the time the door clicked shut, I was in Jim's arms. He met me halfway across the room. It was the only thing we could do. He held me and whispered, "Reena ... I love you more than life itself."

When there were footsteps outside the door, Jim said, "Let them find us like this ..." But suddenly the sounds faded down the hall in a rush, and then we heard the explosion.

"God, no!" Jim cried. "Could it be ...?"

Smoke began pouring in from the adjoining office where the janitor had been cleaning, and we staggered out into the hallway, choking and stumbling into Hal and Nadine, who shouted, "What happened? Was there a bomb? Did you see anyone?"

Jim grabbed Tarrington's arm. "Hal! George!"

"Old George? Old George was in there?"

"I'm sure I heard him moving around before … just before the explosion!"

The smoke was filling the hallway then, and we could hardly breathe, but Jim and Hal broke down the door and dragged out the half-charred body of Old George, the janitor. It was a horrible sight. Nadine screamed endlessly, and Hal just stood over the ruined body, wiping away his tears.

The fire trucks came, and the police and a doctor from a nearby building, but it was too late. They covered George with a white canvas. It was not until morning the next day, after things had been secured, that we saw the place where Jim and Hal had gone through the door. In the center, broken now by the force of their blow, was a splintered, scarlet mark, a jagged cross of half-dried human blood.

We dreaded speaking of it, how our few silent moments together after Hal and Nadine left the office had taken the murderer to the next door, where he heard movement, perhaps the sound of Old George muttering to himself about some dust he couldn't reach with his broom, how we were spared because of the old man's presence in that room.

Nadine jumped on the idea, more true than she could know. "It is that black Dakimu, whose story Jim will not write, who is behind everything!"

And Jim defended him. "You hated him from the beginning, Nadine! Did you want him to leave me to die in the jungle?"

"Does it matter which jungle you die in?" she hissed.

"Just leave it alone, Nadine."

"I want that black picked up. We'll see who is right."

But through all the fear that we faced day and night, the uncertainty, the threats of violence, Jim never believed the murderous hand to be Dakimu's.

Colonel Hahlos lived. The newspapers carried the apology but not the retraction that Edmunde wanted. He was satisfied to have his life and made no more demands.

The assassin waited.

✟   ✟   ✟

One morning, I answered the phone as I passed Liv's empty desk. I did not know the voice, but I jotted down the message. *Press Conference, Colonel Hahlos, Century Life Hotel Banquet Room, 8 p.m. Tuesday.* Jim read over my shoulder.

"Ask who's calling," he said.

But the phone went dead. I replaced the receiver slowly. Jim was mumbling, "Everything is such a goddamn mystery." He slammed his hand down on the desk. "Why doesn't he just say, 'This is your enemy speaking. Come or else I'll bomb the whole damn building!'"

"It sounded legitimate, Jim."

"You mean not like those footsteps outside the door the night they killed Old George instead of us?" he quipped.

"We might as well see what Hahlos is up to," I said, rubbing my hands into the knots in his shoulders.

He relaxed a little and said, "It kills me how many years I have gone without the touch of your hands."

"Never again, my love," I whispered.

"Do you think it's a farewell appearance?" he asked.

"I hope so, for his sake ..." I went on, "Did you know I saw him in Africa before I left?"

"No! What happened?"

"He would tell me nothing," I said, "about you or Dak or the CFA. I hated him so much then."

Jim nodded. "I know he used me. I had the camera and the knowledge of how to travel in the country—lot of good it did me—and I knew some of the language, but I wanted the story, too. I guess he's sorry now I took my job so seriously."

He laughed a little, and then the light went out of his eyes.

"Well, we'll go, of course. Maybe he'll give us some straight answers after all."

"That'll be a first," I said.

"Stay close to me."

"Always."

✢   ✢   ✢

I sat between Jim and Hal, Nadine on the other side of Jim, busy with her notebook and prodding him with suggestions.

"I think we should use the Rolex. There's a good shot of Senator Aimes! You ought to interview some of these people, Jim. See what they really think of Hahlos. Look, there's Sonya! How did she get in? And Merna Stendall! Hasn't she aged? I wonder where Lloyd is. He was never one for these political confrontations, probably out with his mistress, poor Merna!"

When she wasn't looking, Jim squeezed my hand, and once he leaned over and said, "I love you," and Hal heard him and smiled. It was an impressive crowd, almost five hundred people jammed into a room designed for two hundred, and more loitering around outside. A few blacks jostled reporters for front-row seats, but they were treated with patience, although they were closely watched by the cordon of police and FBI agents that lined the room. Everyone was checked for weapons upon entering the room, even the women, but the feeling was that it didn't make any difference. If Hahlos was doomed, the assassin would find a way.

At five minutes before eight, small talk faded, chairs began to creak with the restlessness of their occupants, cameras whirred, and Colonel Hahlos strode vigorously into the room. There was a brief smattering of applause. He was not a popular man now, but you had to respect him for twice defying death to defend his views and his actions. He looked like an ox, sleeked and fattened for show. There was no trace of misery in those ravishing blue eyes that were now steel-like, only hidden anger and intolerance of the situation in which he found himself in a country that had at first greeted him warmly.

"My friends," he began somewhat sarcastically, waving aside the men who were rising to introduce him. "I do not have a lot to say. I will not let them bore you with introductions. If you don't know who I am, you shouldn't be here!"

He was still the proud, embittered man that had sent me away into the

African night without an answer. And I knew he would give no answer to these people whom he had deceived, the blacks who had offered him immunity from death, a safe passage from their forest prison to bring peace to East Africa, the whites who trustingly gave him their arms and ammunition toward that same end. What could he say to appease both of these groups? To pay for the lives that were wasted in the Massacre? To save his own bleak life?

And the answer that came crashing into the smoldering room was: nothing! There was nothing he could say or do, and that is when I knew he would die. White or black, it did not matter; the hand of the assassin approached, and no one would cry for Hahlos. All his present courage in the face of danger could not erase those words, "I have nothing to say to you!" or redeem the sign that should have made us brothers but made us enemies instead … the mark on his arm.

He finished as quickly and as bravely as he had begun. "And now I bid you, in my African tongue, *kwa heri*, good-bye. I go to England, to the home shore that perhaps I should never have left, but did, in the pursuit of peace. I have only one more thing to say as I stand before you, brothers, black and white!"

And he boomed out in a fearful, breaking voice, "I do not apologize for what I am! If you judge me, first judge your own hearts, and if you find an impediment there, a cancer of hate or greed far less than mine, then know that I welcome the death you say I deserve! I swear to you by this mark!"

And he rolled up his sweat-stained, wrinkled shirt and revealed to all the mottled, blistered mark, the cross he never loved, the cross he would die because of but never for, the cross of the Vitani.

And we never saw him again. It was like a dream. He passed along the front row, by his true brothers of the mark, and bent again when he saw my face, taking in Jim's remorseless stare and suddenly remembering, and straightening, and screaming as the bullet of the last brother, the dark, unfathomable one, hidden, as ravaged as the cross he bore, rammed into his heart.

Jim caught him before he hit the floor, and I, too, heard his final words, "What have I done?" And his life, at last, betrayed him.

He was taken from us and from the room, dead. No one moved, strangely, or tried to find the murderer in their midst. It was a small tribute to the man who had just defied them. It made him a hero of sorts, a tragic hero. The play was over; the crowd was stunned, a splendid performance! But no applause this time, no further recognition backstage, no flowers in the dressing room, only on his grave.

Nadine was unappeasable. She swore they were after her, they wanted to hurt Jim for the *Memoirs*, they wanted to scare her into not writing her stories, oh, a hundred reasons, and none of them even close to the truth, if any of us knew the truth. It was Hal who guided her patiently through the stricken crowd to their car in the still quiet parking lot, who calmed her and listened to her and made the suggestion, finally, that saved us.

"Nadine," we heard him say, as we walked behind them arm in arm. "You need a vacation, someplace away from here, someplace private, like my little retreat on the Sound. Why don't you take a couple of weeks and go up there? We can handle your work load. Right, Jim?" he said, glancing back at us.

"Of course," Jim answered, his breath coming heavily in his throat. "I think it's a good idea."

"Well," she said, still shaken but with her voice under control, "I'll think about it."

She and Hal were already in the car, so they could not have seen the shapeless figure in the dark, beside the deserted exit. He slipped once, mistakenly, past the pale red rays of the lighted sign, and we saw his face, twisted, unyielding stone painted black—the face of Dakimu.

✝   ✝   ✝

Nadine went away and Jim came to me in my hotel room. He took my face in his hands and looked at me for achingly long minutes. Finally we both said in the same breath, "Not yet." We sat down on the sofa I had turned around to face the view of the imperious city with a speck of the Atlantic glimmering on a clear day. "It's not the Indian Ocean," Jim said.

"No … but maybe, someday, we'll be there again," I said to comfort him. "Even the desert mirages where I lived so many years always brought that beautiful sea to mind. And you, of course," I added.

"It's funny," he went on quietly, although I could see the stress in his eyes. "I kept that news photo that I thought was you in my wallet for years. One day I gave my wallet to Liv to make a copy of my passport, and she connected that picture with the missionary girl I wrote about in *Memoirs*. When she handed it back she said, 'I didn't mean to pry, but the clipping fell out. I am so sorry, Jim.' I assured her I didn't mind, that I was glad someone knew, that it made it more real. And now, with you right here, I can't make it real."

"You will. I can wait. Just because Nadine is out of town doesn't mean you're not married to her. Her feelings count, too."

"Reena, I am never letting you go."

I clung to those words, but did not know where our ultimate refuge would be.

"And Dak?" I asked.

"I don't blame him for hating me. If I had stopped before I put my pen to the page, not written a word, exposed to light those negatives and burned away the evidence, many lives might have been spared. I might have saved one of those black hearts. I might have saved my friendship with that one black heart. But I let him go back to Africa believing I would print Hahlos' damned three M's. I couldn't love him enough. I only had love for you, and you were gone. So I wrote *Memoirs* while the Massacre raged and Dakimu learned how to kill ... to kill!"

"Jim, he made his own choices."

"And still makes them, as reprehensible as they might be. I denied it, but now I have to face it. It's his hand that wields the gun. It's his bullet in Hahlos' heart. It's his bomb in the body of Old George. His rage in the mark of the cross. But I'll free him from that rage. I'll hold that black skin against my own, that black arm, and make those crosses one!"

Oh, Jim, I cried silently. *You can't. It's too late. There is no cross to share. It's gone, all gone. There are only his words, "What must be, must be," and the massacred flesh on his arm where the cross used to be.* But I could not tell him. I could not say those words.

We slept for a while wrapped in each other's arms. Waking once, Jim asked, "Do you think Dak will listen to me, Reena?"

"I don't know, Jim. I don't know him anymore. I think you should stay away from that wild black arm!"

"But I am imprisoned by it. Don't you see?"

"Yes, I see, and it terrifies me, that vengeful black arm!"

"Can you be afraid of someone and love him at the same time?" he asked.

"I wouldn't have thought so ... before I met Dakimu," I answered, putting Jim's hand against my heart. "But it's a hell of a way to live life for life itself."

He smiled, and we watched the orange-gold light of a New York dawn fill the room.

☩   ☩   ☩

We ate a little breakfast, and I questioned Jim some about his time with Dak. He admitted that he got the photos out of Africa by lying to Dak, saying his cameras had been stolen, when he had already hidden them and was able to retrieve all his notes, everything, before they left the Vitani camp.

He said, "Dak protected me while I deceived him. When I was the sickest I have ever been, he held me. That's something you don't forget. So I decided in the end not to use his name in my book. But it wasn't enough. He took my betrayal to heart, and so here we are on a collision course. I can only guess at what he did to save me from Kisasi. He must have promised to go back, to lead the Massacre, to give them the missing pieces of the Council's plans, most of which he got from me! The places to find weapons, tribes that would fight for him or against him, the names of his white enemies. But why? Why did he promise to go back?"

"He loved his people, Jim. He found something in those hills that we couldn't give him. He must have longed for it."

"As I longed for you! But what happened to his faith in God, your Christian God?" Jim asked, and then he said, "It's something I never found anyway."

"You are the same man, with or without Him," I answered. "And He is the same God."

✛   ✛   ✛

The sound of the telephone jarred us. Jim turned away from me reluctantly and answered it, holding it so I could hear the voice at the other end.

"Hello?" Jim said cautiously.

"Strange that you should answer," said Dakimu Reiman. "Isn't that a little risky?"

"Not anymore," Jim said. "I'm leaving Nadine. Why did you call, Dak?"

"To talk to Reena ... but you'll do."

"That's good, because I want to talk to you."

"I thought you might want that interview now."

"What interview?"

"With me, for the story you are doing."

"We're not going to write it now, Dak."

"You're not ... going to write it? Why?"

Jim looked at me, and then said softly into the phone, "I think you know why, Dakimu. And the fact that I am here with Reena should tell you more."

"Well, I have something to tell you! It's too late. It doesn't matter whether you write it or not! I am being hunted by the police and who knows who else, but this place is a maze, and I have eluded them. They are getting close though, Jim. They are moving in. And I want out! *Nakwenda kwetu.* I am going home. And I want your help."

"My help?"

"Yes. Yours and Reena's, too. You owe it to me."

"We paid our debt, Dakimu."

"How?"

"By keeping silent."

"That is not enough. You must help me! Now listen. I am only five blocks from you. The whole street is alive with cops. They don't know

I'm here, but it won't take them long. I have another hole in this jungle, where other friends shall save me. They have ways with airline officials. *Means*, you know, Jim, means to an end? But I need you to get me there … today."

"I will come …"

"You must walk, all the way. Any car they study with extreme suspicion. A man on foot is no threat, and you probably won't be recognized in this district. You will simply be a tenant coming home for lunch."

"Lunch?"

"Yes … you must be here at twelve noon, for the rest of the plan to work."

Jim's chest was heaving, and sweat poured down his face as he asked, "Why noon?"

He almost whispered, "You'll have to trust me."

"And you will have to tell me one more thing, Dak, or I won't come."

"Make it quick!"

"Where am I taking you?"

"Oh, hell, why shouldn't you know … to the basement locker room at Kennedy Airport. There are some small offices and storage rooms. I shall wait in number 3 for the plane that will take me home."

"And, Dak, whatever you are planning, leave Reena out of it!"

There was a thoughtful silence before he said, "She has been out of it for a long time, Jim. This is between you and me. What I said about her help meant only this. She must let you go! She must let you come to me … at the appointed time!"

There was a click and a dull, heartless tone and then silence, as Jim replaced the receiver. "Jim?"

"Oh God," he breathed, and it was not a curse, as he had called that name when we first met. It was a prayer.

"Jim, what can I do?"

"Let me go. Let me go to Dak. And then we shall be free of him. I love you, Reena … and I can't live without you. But neither can I live in a prison of fear. When Dak is gone, this fear, too, will rise with him into the African sky. Let him have his pain … I am done with it."

And it was eleven o'clock.

We dared not remember, but we did, just before Jim left, that it was the same hour I had gone to find him in Africa, when he did not come back to see me or say good-bye, and I was left with nothing but a few memories and the sweet, black hand of Dakimu Reiman, guiding me across the land. Jim walked out the door without a backward glance ... and there was no time for good-bye.

"I love you!" I called down the stairway, and he straightened his shoulders and moved more surely toward his rendezvous, and still he did not look back.

✛　✛　✛

I got in Jim's car and drove slowly down the street. It was half past twelve. The streets seemed deserted—no laughing children, no mothers with guarded eyes, no roaming dogs or bony cats or beggars. I was alone in Jim's shining, azure car. Like the sky. Today the sky stretched across the building tops, the leafless trees, the empty streets, as one unmarred sea-blue canvas, waveless, windless, serene. And except for one white winging dove, it was empty, too.

I had almost gone the five blocks, when from out of the innocent air, there came a sound that shattered my heart, that stirred the small, calm breezes into whirlwinds, that ripped the very breath out of my lungs—the explosion of trigger and hammer and fire and steel, the cry of one doomed spirit, the crash of the running feet of the dark assassin, the squeal of the tires and brakes beneath my own feet, as I came to a stop in the blood-drenched street beside the broken, lifeless body of Jim Stone.

Eusi

Her book is closed. She can write no more, not because she does not know the end, but because I am the only one who can speak of it. I could go back, to the night in Reena's room when she realized what I meant to do, to the hour that Hahlos knew my sweet revenge, to the morning that my enemies at Peacetime Publications drew me with my bomb, but I shall go on … from the afternoon that I shot Jim Stone.

+ + +

He came on time, moving at a natural gait up the street, easily, confidently, and no one questioned him. He turned into my building at twelve o'clock and knocked at my door. I felt his hand pounding on my heart.

"Come in," I said.

He walked through the door.

"Jim, you're right on time."

"What do you want me to do?"

"What? No conversation?"

"I thought you were in a hurry."

"Oh, there is a little time, Jim, just a little … Sit down."

"I'll stand," he said.

I shrugged and came to the point. "Jim, there is one thing I want to know from you."

He stood there so calmly, so fearlessly, that I hesitated to speak. *Why not take out the gun and have it over with?* But I asked, "How did you get the pictures? How did you get them out of Africa?"

He told me about the bedroll, about the camera no bigger than his hand that had all the photographs of the big camera, in case I found that one, about his lies to me. "And for these things," he said, "I have no defense."

Then I said, looking straight into his eyes, "Is there anything you wish to ask me?"

"Why?"

"Before I kill you …"

The amazing thing was that his eyes did not change. They stared back at me, still unafraid, and all I could say was, "You knew?"

He nodded.

What must be, must be. I wondered if he had ever seen those words inscribed in Reena's copy of his *Memoirs*. But there was no time for more questions. The car that would carry me to safety was due.

"Jim," I said, barely able to speak now. "Do you forgive me?"

His eyes never left my face. "Do you … forgive me?"

It was an answer for both of us—his final question, his dying blow to my own black heart.

"It must be out there, Jim," I said, pointing to the street.

He turned and opened the door to his death, moved quickly to the black-tarred and guttered jungle and turned again, so he would see my poisoned spear pierce his heart.

He fell. My car was coming. But still I did not move. I knew Reena would follow him, and I was ready. But I was not ready for the look on her face or her one incandescent plea: "I want to go with him!"

The automatic was, in my aching hand, still warm, and I lowered it to the ground.

"No!" she commanded with her eyes, her heart, her very life.

"Now!" she cried, my love, my angel, my destroyer.

"Now!" she wept, my Juliet, my Christ, my Africa.

"Now!" she screamed, ten feet and a world away, and I lifted my arm, slowly, through the ages that man has made war on man, nation has slaughtered nation, brother has murdered brother, to this pure, final, agonizing act, and pulled the trigger ...

Black

This is the way I had planned it. This is the way I had imagined it all these years, my last bullets fired into their hearts, but when they stood at my door at the hour of our beginning, I suddenly loved them so much I could not find the strength, the anger, to finish it. They stood there with such innocence and trust, even suspecting what I might do, such belief in my love that I put the gun in their hands and said, "Do with me what you will."

"We'll take you to storeroom number 3," they said. "The cops will follow the car that is coming for you, not ours."

And that's what they did.

✤　✤　✤

I write from my village in Africa, still called Huzuni, and filled with refugees from wars and struggles that have nothing to do with Reena and Jim. It was never their battle, and they are free now. I no longer call myself a Christian, but I let the missionaries come and set up shop in the forest and listen to their words, and though I do not believe, I feel redemption in my part of Reena and Jim's salvation. I kept them apart; I brought them together.

As for the rest, I am not sorry.

White

After we left Dak in the storeroom, we took the gun to a river that shall not be named and threw it in. It seemed our last tie to Africa and even to God, so crushed were our hearts losing our black friend in such a way.

Nadine, who had returned from Hal's days early, was so wary of the whole thing, her murder suspect disappearing and Jim and I walking into the office distraught and clinging to each other, that there could be no repairing of their relationship.

She did not contest the divorce. In fact, she said she was glad to be rid of that *whole mess* with that black. We all went on working on the story, following police leads and odd sightings of the African, Jim and I smiling to ourselves, while Nadine hired extra security at home and office. We told Hal in confidence that our black friend was no longer a threat. After a few days he stopped all research projects on Dak, saying that the authorities had informed him the black was out of the country. Everyone but Nadine breathed a sigh of relief.

"He ruined our lives," she said one day. "Jim was never the same, after he came back to London with that man!"

If she knew I was the missionary girl Jim had written about in *Memoirs*, she never let on.

✢　✢　✢

Jim spent another night with me before his divorce was final, but we talked
until morning, remembering Africa with its endless plains and deep forests,
the black people with whom we had felt safe and loved, and the ones, black
and white, who had threatened and scared us. We turned on the radio and
danced dangerously close, but we did not give in to our desire. Jim wanted
to read to me from the first pages of *Memoirs*. Hearing his voice speak those
words was almost like making love.

*I woke in a white room in a white bed, with morning light streaming
through filmy white drapes, filling the shadows in the room, and the shadows
in my mind. Something wasn't right. I could barely lift my hand to reach the
glass of water on a small table nearby. The blankets pressed a terrible weight
on my chest, but still I shivered, as though I had not been warm for a long
time. That bleak sunlight pouring into the place where I lay was as foreign as
the clean sheets and bare walls around me. When I tried to raise my head, the
room swirled, ever darkening and throwing me out of balance.*

*Then, I knew suddenly what the strangeness was. The sun's rays did not
touch me through the lens of Africa. I was no longer in the land I loved. I was
suffering on the edge of a dreary, white world to which I did not belong, and
I knew, still hazy and half-afraid, what I had to do. I had to tell the story of
all the other mornings, the African mornings, a story of terror and joy, violence
and beauty, a story I had promised someone I wouldn't write, a story of another
I lost along the way, whose light seems to have been extinguished, as I lay in
this cold, safe place.*

An insignia on a tray that I could now turn my head to see said, Crestwood
Clinic, London, England, *and I began to remember more. I remembered
strong, black arms carrying me through the doors, a shrill woman, my wife,
ordering people around, and a pain in my entire being that dwelled just at the
surface, waiting to assail me. I remembered my name, Jim Stone, and that the
story had begun almost ten years before, when I stepped on a plane at midnight
in England and disembarked on the Dark Continent under a blazing sun.*

I was twenty-four. I'd been given an assignment for the London Free
Press, *mostly because no one else was interested in reporting on the rumors of
dissatisfaction with British rulers in the little-known country of Tanganyika.
I had been married for five years, everyone said, "way too young," and they*

were right. I had been drawn to a woman several years older who was a striking beauty and already respected in the field of journalism. But I soon wearied of her controlling nature and even the sound of her voice. We agreed the separation might save us, but instead of falling more in love with her, I fell in love with Africa.

When I arrived in 1950, there were a lot of white people in the country. They were busy "colonizing," killing big-game animals, and enslaving the natives with innocuous titles like "house servant" and "field hand." I was not content to write about the dealings of white men in a country clearly not their own. I sought out natives, speaking to them at first with a translator and then in my own halting Swahili. Many of them thought I only meant to do them harm. It challenged me.

I had never touched a skin other than white. Admittedly, I was anxious, but the first time I took a black hand, a spark of recognition passed between us that I will never forget. It was not as simple as this is another human being who happens to have a different skin color, *but our hearts connected. I had come to Africa hungry to report the differences. But soon, I longed for the sameness: the struggle to survive and love, the need for companionship and loyalty.*

All those things came quite early in my experience, because I fell ill with malaria. The white doctors tired of my visits to their clinics, half-dead from the ravages of the mosquito-borne virus. Who healed me were the blacks. When I was at my lowest, unable to eat or drink, it was black arms who lifted me from despair. It was black faces that leaned over me, black hands that offered tribal medicines and simple comfort. It was their dreams and their heartbreaks I would tell, not knowing that my own dreams and heartbreaks would be inextricably bound to theirs or that one black would give me the greatest gift, and then take it away, as if wanting me to pay for the transgressions of my people.

He swallowed hard and closed the book. He could read no more.

✛   ✛   ✛

Then came the night we were free. It was stormy, with a strangely warm breeze, like the nights we spent in separate rooms on the Indian Ocean. Jim laid the legal papers with Nadine's signature where I could see it.

"I am sorry, if I hurt her," he said. "But I'm not sorry I fell in love with you."

And joyfully beyond joy, we made love for the first time. We had ached for that hour, but it was edged with unknowing. So much time and so much pain had gone before. Yet we fit like nothing we had ever imagined, every move transporting us to a higher plane, every move filled with our African passion, every move an answer to the question raised in the dark hallway of Jim's apartment in Dar es Salaam, every move a place we were now not afraid to go. Now heart to heart, instead of hand to heart, we celebrated our love.

"Reena Pavane, I am now saved," he said, caressing my bare shoulders, kissing my face wet with tears, and making love to me again.

✢   ✢   ✢

Jim and I travel and write and long for Africa and shudder in each other's arms at the way it could have ended. Dakimu is still with us, his secrets, his beautiful face, our crosses reminding us daily of his hatred and his love, while his cross fades away with time.

But some things never fade, the terrible and glorious images of Africa imprinted on our souls, the Africa that seals us forever in an uncommon bond.

PEACETIME PUBLICATIONS
NEW YORK CITY
NEW YORK 10016

ATTN: JIM STONE
REENA PAVANE

5¢

in H.
my deepest gratitude
D.

White and Black

✧ ✦ ✧

After twenty years, we went back to the land of our joy and our pain. We rented a jeep in Dar es Salaam and drove the one hundred miles to Huzuni. Dak did not know we were coming, but we knew he was there.

Every mile was a healing, the green and enigmatic canopied forests full of music and life, the acacia savannah more peaceful than it had been for a time. Villagers came out to greet us as if there had never been a Council for Africa or a massacre. The colors soothed our eyes, the sounds blessed our ears, the river crossings humbled us and allowed us passage.

Finally we pulled into the clearing at Huzuni where Jim had drawn me away to the helicopter so many years ago. A new cross stood in the field. Children came to see us, dancing in the afternoon, no matter we were strangers. And then, there was Dak walking toward us with astonished eyes, saying, "At last ... at last." And he took us in his arms, holding us ever closer to his heart and whispering in a choked voice, "In all my life ... I have loved only you."

And Christ on the cross tore one hand through the nails
and reached His arm out to us through the hallowed African light ...

Though the cause of evil prosper,
Yet 'tis truth alone is strong;
Truth forever on the scaffold,
Wrong forever on the throne,
Yet that scaffold sways the future,
And, behind the dim unknown,
Standeth God within the shadow
Keeping watch above his own ...

—James Russell Lowell, 1844

·

PART TWO

Found History—Tanzania, 1985

✧   ✦   ✧

For as long as I can remember, my father has been wanted for murder. I am almost thirty, and I have never seen him, nor does he know I exist. I was born in the camp of the Vitani during the Massacre, when my country was still called Tanganyika. My father was a great warrior and seldom home in my village. He had forsaken my mother, who bore my sister by another man. For this betrayal, he had ravaged her, and I was conceived. She never told him. As for my mother, she is not retarded exactly but becomes oddly confused and agitated over the smallest thing. But about this, she is quite sure. I am that renowned black man's son.

Now she has been summoned to trial in Dar es Salaam as a witness against him for the recent slaying of two white men, and I may be asked to stand up also. What can I say? I don't know him. My head is filled with the stories my mother told me and what I learned from faded news clippings. I long for this man, to see him, to touch him, as if that would make me real. I have lived on the edge of dreams but never been in the dreams of the warrior who created me. This cries for resolution. But what will my father do with me?

My name is Kiiku, some letters taken from my grandfather's name and some from my father's. My mother's father was the king of many tribes who made war with whites and Christians, black and white, for decades. He was fierce and undefeatable, except by the hand of death, which came while my father was at his side. I was still in my mother's womb. The king was buried, and my father ran away to a foreign land where it is said he continued to kill, if one can believe the reports.

It is also said that here in Africa he cared deeply for a white man as a friend. I cannot imagine this. I spoke to few white people at university but only to be polite. I could never love one. It is hinted by some that a white woman had his heart, and this he will have to tell me himself, because that idea is beyond recognition. If it is true, I will search for that woman like a lion for an eland calf. I must unearth the darkest secrets of my father's life, since I am one of them and the only one I know.

My mother is making preparations for our journey. She stares out at the forest trail, as if she doesn't comprehend where she is. Will she testify with gentleness or with wrath? Even these concepts are beyond her. I was raised by native nursemaids and then raised my sister myself. She was one year older but soon fell behind and never passed the threshold of twelve. I didn't mind, as the villagers avoided her, and she was a sweet girl who sang to the stars and wandered happily outside in the long rains. She died some years ago, drowned in the river beside our camp on a clear spring day. I was the only one who shed tears. My mother never said who her father was. I was glad I had befriended her. No one should walk in the world alone.

The day of our appearance in Dar es Salaam looms like the obelisks of the high plateaus of Ethiopia in the far north, our place in the mystery of my father a carved message in stone that no one can read. A few days before we leave, my mother puts a book in my hands. It is red with deeply etched gold lettering on the front that reads: *Memoirs on an African Morning*. It was written by a white journalist twenty-five years ago. What does it have to do with me?

"Book ... book," my mother says a little desperately.

I flip through the pages. There are stunning photos of forests and savannahs and waterfalls and disturbing ones of war atrocities and village poverty. There are pictures of ritual dance ceremonies that no white man would ever be allowed to view. I skim the words, becoming angry at phrases like "Africa is my home, my destroyer and my savior" and "The Black, my friend, put his arms around me and held me until the pain subsided." What kind of nonsense is this? And then I am stopped cold by: "I was in the prison of King Kisasi for 348 days." King Kisasi—my grandfather.

I sling the book to the ground. My mother screams when she finds that precious volume in the ochre dust. She wipes it clean like she would a fine treasure, with soft strokes. I have never received such a caress from her. I hate the book and covet the book at the same time. Its images cannot become mine, nor its language, in a fleeting glimpse of truths I was heartlessly denied.

Finally we are on our way to the judicial magistrate in the matter of my father's crime. It is a two-day trek by jeep, which has been supplied by the whites who want to cut his throat. They chatter away. Do they think I don't understand English?

"Yeah, he's guilty all right. Two white guys gunned down in the middle of the night a couple of miles from where he says he was visiting friends!"

"Nobody else up there that night, according to the tire tracks, and he goes missing the next day!"

"He did turn himself in though."

"Yeah, because he thinks his white friends will cover for him, under oath. That'll never happen."

"Not much chance for that renegade!"

I twist my hands together to keep from striking them. I love my father even more in those moments. My mother does not move or say a word.

✛   ✛   ✛

We arrive in the late evening and are escorted to a spacious room in a clean hotel overlooking the Indian Ocean, an azure plain stretching away into the unknown. My mother sleeps, but I do not. She has placed the red book on the nightstand, but I do not open it.

The next day, we are taken to the courthouse, and it feels like the first day of my life. The room is overflowing with spectators and reporters. We are seated so far back that I can barely understand what is happening. I choke back my anxiety. Mother's eyes are closed. But suddenly I see what

I have yearned for forever—a tall black man perhaps in his early fifties approaching the stand. He is so beautiful I restrain a gasp. It is my father. His hand is on the Bible.

"Dakimu, do you swear ..."

My mother had said he was a Christian once, but now he glances defiantly at the gathering, as if that text under his hand is a burden. I try to make him notice me, but there are too many of us—black, white, and brown in a collage of unfamiliar and hostile faces. Everyone is standing except my mother, who does not register the impact of the proceedings.

I try to imagine what is in my father's head. Has he killed those two men in self-defense but will say he knows nothing of it? He is answering questions now, but I am more mesmerized by his voice than by what he is revealing. It is pure heaven, the sound of my father's voice quieting the room. He is self-assured and well-spoken. He is fearless and believable. He is not going to suffer for the death of those whites.

"And you continue to maintain you were with friends at their home not far from the scene at the time of the shooting?" the prosecutor is asking.

"Yes."

"Are these friends here?"

"Yes."

"Will you point them out?"

My father spreads out his arms as if to embrace three figures in the front row—a younger black woman, a white woman about his age leaning toward a white man several years older. When he looks at them, they become one person. They become his passion, his joy, his hope. He knows nothing of me.

Then the judge motions each of them to the witness box, beginning with the white woman who is sworn in as Reena Pavane. What poetry in that name and in her fleeting grip of my father's shoulder as she passes by him. And when she turns and faces us, I am shattered with one more truth about my father. This is the woman he has loved. She is lovely, calm, and steady in her lie: "He was at my home at nine o'clock for dinner and did not leave until two a.m. the next morning."

The room is startled to silence. And I think I am the only one there,

I who know so little, who knows why she lied. My father nods at her as she returns to her chair, and their connection feels like lightning arcing between two dark clouds.

The white man, Jim Stone, is questioned about his *Memoirs*. So *he* is the author of the red book! I smile. Mother lifts her head for the first time at the mention of his name. He recounts the same story with the same studied lie. And I realize he is the one my father held through some unbearable pain years ago. I find myself not being able to hate him.

The young black woman also says she was with my father, but she hesitates a bit and falters on the lie. The prosecutor pushes her until she sobs, "I was in the car, but he shoved me to the back seat, and I saw nothing after that."

Oh, treachery. My heart breaks. I have not been called yet, but I stand now and make my way through the babbling crowd to the table where my father rests with his head in his hands, to our unheralded reparation.

And Ye Shall Go Out with Joy

✧　◆　✧

W hen the white people came into the emergency room, I didn't
know what to think. Our little Catholic hospital was known to
serve blacks in that part of Dar es Salaam. What were they doing here? The
man appeared to be having a heart attack. I couldn't turn them away.

"Please help us!" the woman cried out.

In behind them strode the most beautiful black African I had ever
seen. He must have driven them here, not knowing where else to go in his
own country.

"My friend has been ill with malaria," the black man said, "but now
we think his heart is compromised."

Perfect English, soft-spoken, a slight desperation hidden.

"Of course … I'll call a doctor," I said with a professional air.

Who were they? I led them to the chairs. The white man seemed about
to collapse. He was ashen-faced and having difficulty breathing.

"How far have you come?" I asked.

"One hundred miles," the white woman replied, holding the white
man with all of her strength. "We were just married," she said. "It's a very
special day for us."

They were not young. She maybe late forties, he sixty. But it didn't
seem a usual *special day*. It seemed a milestone of some sort in a long
relationship. Then I got the shock of my life.

She said, "I'm Reena Pavane."

189

I didn't tell them right away. I let it sink deep into my being, my knowledge of who I was, because that was my name, too. I was named after a white missionary who loved my people and brought them to the Lord in the 1950s. As I write this, it is 1985.

The doctor rushed in with a gurney, and the white man was wheeled away. Reena Pavane fell into the black man's arms. There was something there, too, between them. I was afraid to know.

"I'll be back," I whispered, unsure of my own voice, and followed the ill white man through the sliding doors to the exam room.

"This is Jim Stone," Doctor Mbulu said. "He's recently arrived from the United States and has been visiting a friend in Huzuni."

My heart lurched again. That was where my mother learned about Jesus! The village suffered through a terrible massacre in the sixties and was rebuilt only a few years ago. There were atheists and Christians living in the same community but without violence, without dread of militant drums in the night. I crossed myself. I was not at ease with white people, and now I had seen a handsome African consoling Reena Pavane with great tenderness. I stepped out of Mr. Stone's room and went back to my destiny.

They were still sitting quite close together. Maybe they were praying. The black looked up and smiled and offered one hand. The other held the white woman's hand to his heart.

"I am Dakimu Reiman," he said.

"We're doing some tests and giving him some fluids. You should be able to see him soon." I turned away, still embarrassed by their closeness.

"Don't go," this Dak ... imu said softly. "I need to find us some food. Would you be kind enough to stay with Mrs. Stone?"

"I can stay for a short time," I said, wanting desperately to be needed elsewhere.

Then Reena Pavane looked at me. I was the one with the gold cross around my neck. She was the one with the love. I sat down, and the beautiful black leaned over and kissed her face.

"Are you uncomfortable with us?" She paused and then said, "We have been friends and ... well, friends, for a very long time. That's all."

"White people don't come to this hospital," I told her by way of answering.

"I understand. But know that Africa has been our first home, our first love, you might say. We feel we belong here, in spite of the color of our skin. I'm sorry if it offends you."

"No ... really, it's not that ... Oh, Mrs. Stone, I must tell you ... I was named for you. I am Reena Pavane."

Her eyes shone. "Oh, my dear, how ...?"

"My mother lived in Huzuni. She always loved you. She came to Dar es Salaam after you left but couldn't let go of the girl who led her to God, so here I am ... with your name."

"And your mother?"

"Her name was Luzan. She's dead now."

"Luzan. I remember her. She was the first to accept my family, our beliefs, our color. I'm sorry she's gone."

"And I wanted to be like her, but Catholicism was the best Christianity I could find growing up."

"Bless you. You have found more than most."

Mr. Reiman had returned and given Reena a cold sandwich. He brought me African tea and a small white flower from the hospital gardens. Then he began telling me about them, with Reena Pavane leaning against him, barely able to eat.

"We met before the Massacre," he said, "and spent many troubling years together and apart. We are Africa to each other, the good and the bad. We would give our lives for each other, when once we might have taken a life. We are not used to explaining our past to strangers, but we need your assistance. It is only fair that you should know more than what you see on the surface."

"Of course. I'll do what I can," I said.

Dr. Mbulu was standing in the doorway. "You may come in now," he said.

I was going to let them go without me, but Dakimu gestured that I should stay with them. Mr. Stone turned his face as we entered, and I was glad to see he looked much better. Dakimu went quickly to his side and laid his hand on the white man's forehead. It seemed a blessing, as though the black was the priest and Mr. Stone the sinner. But no, the white man had such passion in his eyes it drew tears from the black. Reena kissed her husband on the lips with that black hand hovering faithfully over them. I straightened the sheets and poured a glass of water to be useful.

"Jim," Reena said, "this young lady has my name! Her mother's home was in Huzuni when I was a teenager."

"Reena," he said and smiled. I had to admit he was very good-looking, even though he was not at his best.

"Yes ... I never imagined I would meet your wife. I understood she had left Africa some time ago."

"And so she did, but we were drawn back ... for many reasons. If you wish to know more, I'm sure Dakimu will give a just accounting."

"He has warned me of some uncertain times."

"Yes ... but you see we are one now."

"I do see something ... of grace between you. I envy it. I would not know how to find that without my Church."

"Well, that is a fine place to start, my dear," he said, beginning to tire.

"But you are not Catholic."

"No, but now I am in your hands."

"I think that's enough for him," Dr. Mbulu said, coming into the room.

Mr. Stone appeared to have fallen asleep, but Reena wouldn't leave him. Dakimu and I walked down the hall. It was the end of my shift, but I wanted to keep walking with this strange and beautiful man who only had heart for Mr. and Mrs. Stone.

"I'm sorry I'm so quiet. You have been solicitous of my friends," he said.

"I'm just trying to figure out what's happened in the last hour."

"Hm ... I've been trying to figure it out for half my life," he said, relaxing a little.

"Half? What did you know before?"

"I knew who I was, what I believed, what I hated, what I dreamed of, lived for."

"And then what happened?"

"I met Reena Pavane."

"And what changed?"

"I wanted to possess her and kill the man she loved."

I said nothing.

"Of course, I did neither, but it transformed me. I took out my despair on a lot of innocent people, maybe some not so innocent. But here I am with Jim and Reena again."

"You love them very much, don't you?"

"I do."

"Why?"

"She gave me spirit. He gave me anger. Together they gave me redemption."

"Only Jesus can do that," I said with conviction.

"He might have a hand in it," he said, smiling briefly.

"How can you speak so ... casually, about something so sacred?"

"The sacred can wound you."

"It can heal you, too."

"Perhaps ... but it hasn't happened yet. Not entirely."

"Would you like to see my priest?"

"Oh, no." He laughed then. "I left all that behind long ago."

"But you don't have to leave it behind forever," I said.

"You are sweet to care, Reena named for Reena," he said. "I might have to give your God a chance, just to please you."

"You may please me, but I could never be what your Reena is to you."

"It's true. I have never considered that anyone could be. I closed myself off from everyone—God, family, pretty girls like you. But there were circumstances."

"Tell me one."

"Hm ... and end this nice chat so soon?"

"Please."

"I ... hurt people."

"We have all hurt people."

"Not in the ways I have." He looked away. "We must not talk about this anymore."

"You could tell my priest," I risked saying.

"I will consider it, Reena Pavane. It's not out of the question. I have wondered what such a man of God would say."

"He is very compassionate, my priest. And he has seen a lot of … wrongdoing."

"I'm glad for you. We all need someone with whom we can bare our hearts. Even my friends, Jim and Reena, don't know everything. But they knew enough years ago to get me safely out of their country before I could be shot dead in the street."

"Oh." I shuddered.

"I have said too much. Please forgive me." He touched the white flower that I had pinned to my uniform. "Think only of pure things and keep your promises to God. I don't think He will let you down."

"I thought you didn't believe in Him."

"Oh, I have called out to Him a time or two. I believe it was He who drew the plane through the air and me back to Africa."

"I'm thankful He did. I never would have met Reena … or you."

I know he wanted to reach out to me, but I didn't trust myself. He was exciting and dangerous. I lived a quiet life of service. My feelings troubled me. But I wanted to know more, so much more.

"Would you like to have dinner?" he asked, looking at me again.

"Tonight?"

"If you will."

"I know a little place," he said, and then smiled briefly, as if remembering a private joke.

I gave him a questioning look.

"Oh, it's something Jim told me once. When he first met Reena, he said that to her, and then added, 'I don't usually use that line on missionaries!' It seems quite fitting that I repeated that to you, another Reena Pavane."

"Shall we take Mrs. Stone?"

"I'm sure Mrs. Stone is quite happy where she is. She and Jim were separated for many years and found each other by accident. I played my part, but what they have together is … well, holy. I don't mean that in a religious sense," he said quickly. "It's hard to define."

We left the hospital, and Dak led me down a narrow street to an open-air café.

"Reena and Jim … such devotion," he said.

"I can see it … their passion. But it scares me, too. I am used to a safe, calm life."

"Not anymore," he whispered, and he rested his hand briefly on my arm. "You needn't be afraid of me, Miss Pavane."

"Oh … I'm more afraid of myself. Getting involved where I don't belong, with things I will never understand."

"You don't have to understand to be a part of something foreign to you. How do you imagine Jim and Reena and I maintained our bond?"

"That's another hesitation I have … that when you say my name, you'll be thinking of her."

"It will be a hard habit to break," he admitted.

"If I had a different name, would you have still asked me to dinner?"

"I surely think so," he answered. "Listen, Reena. The three of us existed on different continents for the last twenty-five years, and there was not one day I didn't miss their voices, their touch."

"Especially hers?"

"Maybe … but he and I have a powerful history. I always longed for them as separate individuals, until today."

"What happened today?"

"I married them."

I made the sign of the cross on his chest. He caught my hand. "I am not worthy," he said.

"I believe you are."

"But you don't know …"

"I don't want to know. You should go see Father Amani."

"Perhaps I will …"

We ate in silence then. We had met only a few hours ago but now faced changes in ourselves we had not thought possible. It was sobering. What did we have to lose? We would learn of a different kind of sacrifice, a different kind of love. Perhaps that is what God wanted for us after all.

I left Dakimu at the hospital and drove home, although I didn't want to. The three friends would be together now, and I couldn't know or feel what passed between them. I couldn't hear the voice of the woman for whom I was named or comfort her husband, as I was trained to do, or steal a look at Dakimu as he watched over the two he loved. In the morning, they could even be gone. I said the Lord's Prayer and tried to sleep. I dreamed of Reena Pavane.

At eight o'clock in the morning, I was out the door, though my shift didn't start until ten. I was haunted by Dakimu and his friends, even though I dreaded knowing their story. I seemed to want to *change* their story, and that was so unlike me. Father Amani would help me find my way. Dakimu was coming out of the hospital entrance, and he embraced me but swiftly let go.

"He's all right. Some medication and rest will support him. I'm going to get them a room at the Imperial Arms for a week. Dr. Mbulu doesn't think he should return to Huzuni just yet."

"I worried all night," I said.

"Is that part of your job?" he asked.

"Well … no, but I seem to care uncharacteristically about all of you …" I couldn't say another word.

"I should like to see your priest today," he said.

"You are grateful your friend survived."

"It's more than that," he said. "They came so far to see me, and I love them so, but they love each other more. I feel … empty, disconsolate. What can fill that?"

"Father Amani will know."

"I guess I'll take that chance."

I then touched his hand and said, "I'll drive you to the church at four, when my shift ends."

"Thank you, Reena," he said and went off on his errand.

When I stepped into Jim Stone's room, he was sitting in a chair trying to eat some thin oatmeal. His IV was still in, and I didn't like his color.

Reena was asleep on a bed the staff had pulled over next to her husband's. He put a finger to his lips so I wouldn't wake her, but I had to speak.

"Mr. Stone ..."

"Jim ... please call me Jim."

"Jim, you need to take some deep breaths and let me help you back in that bed."

"But the doctor said he'd release me, if I could sit here for an hour and eat something."

"And how is that going?"

"Not too well, I think."

"Right ... think of your poor wife, exhausted fearing for you."

"Reena ..."

Did he mean me or her? She woke anyway, and we got him back in the bed. I felt he was somewhat feverish, so I went to find the doctor on shift. I was sure Mbulu wasn't in yet, but I was wrong. He was coming down the corridor with another med for Jim.

"His heart's fine. We're having trouble controlling the malarial symptoms. This should relieve him." And he showed me a relatively new drug for malaria. "Would you put this in his IV?"

"Of course, Doctor."

"You're rather attached to them, Miss Pavane," he said.

"Yes," I said. "I don't mean to be."

"'The heart wants what the heart wants,'" he whispered.

Oh, how it does, I thought, going back into Jim's room. Mrs. Stone looked up and smiled. It was hard to call her Reena. She had been such a fantasy in my life. The real woman confounded me.

"Did you see Dak this morning?" she asked.

"Yes, ma'am. He was going to secure you a place to stay for a few days."

"Yes, the Imperial Arms, where Jim and I spent a week in 1957."

"You've been together that long?"

"Together in our hearts but not in life. It took some years to reconnect."

"An answer to prayer, I suppose."

"Something like that," she offered.

"Reena," I said very carefully, trying out the sound of her name.

"Yes?"

"Do you mind if Dakimu visits my priest?"

"Of course not. He seems to need something we can't give him right now. If I could put God back in his heart, I would."

"His heart seems to be filled up with ..." I stopped suddenly.

"With me ... I know. The thing is ... I do love him. I can't deny him that."

"He must make a choice. It's not up to you entirely," I said bravely.

"Your priest ... is he young?" she asked.

"A bit older than Dakimu, I believe."

"That's good. I think for Dak to open up, he needs someone who's been in the Church a long time. When are you going?"

"At the end of my shift, about four-thirty."

"I'll be thinking of you ... both of you. You were courageous to ask him to see a priest. I think that's why he agreed. Thank you."

She squeezed my hand, and I left the room to attend to my duties with a lighter heart, but I could barely concentrate as the day wore on. Patients would ask for something, and I'd forget what it was before I reached the nurses' station. I saw Dakimu go back into Jim's room around three o'clock. I was very attracted to him. Was I meant to be the one to save him from himself? I felt innocent and inadequate, except for my Catholic faith, which had been my anchor.

At four, Dakimu was waiting for me outside the hospital. We drove slowly. The church was only a few blocks away. We were Father's last appointment. We walked up the steps of St. Joseph's Cathedral where the carved wooden doors beckoned with their rich patterns. Dakimu stopped halfway, but I took his hand and drew him with me into the sanctuary. The afternoon light still glimmered through the stained glass. The choir was rehearsing an anthem I had never heard before.

They sang, "Ho, everyone that thirsteth, come ye to the waters ... and ye shall go out with joy." For each of us, the words had such different meanings. We sat in the last pew and waited for Father Amani, letting the music calm the struggle in our hearts.

Soon, Father came out and asked Dakimu how he could help him.

"I don't know. I need to tell someone what I've done."

"Do you wish to tell me here or in the confessional?" Father Amani asked.

"What is the difference?"

"Out here, the world may come to know and judge you. In there, only God and I will know, and there is no judgment."

"It seems an easy choice," Dakimu said quietly.

"It may be the hardest choice you ever make, my son," Father said, guiding him to the confessional.

After a time, I heard weeping and the soothing voice of Father Amani. Tears sprang to my eyes, and I realized I was falling in love with Dakimu Reiman. It seemed that I had known him in my dreams. He filled my emptiness, as he was searching for something to fill his.

He came out and immediately grasped my hand. We went out into the African twilight, which was momentary here on the equator, like Dakimu's peace with what had happened.

"Can you tell me what Father said?" I asked.

"He said I had already been forgiven by God, but I had not yet forgiven myself."

"And how are you to do that?"

"Go and sin no more. Make reparations to the families of those I … harmed. Be very cautious with my passion for Reena. Some impossible tasks, I believe."

"But did Father help you at all?"

"Yes. He was very kind. He did not despise me. He said I could always come back."

"And will you?"

"I will. Some of my pain is relieved, if only by the sound of his voice. It may be a tough climb to 'ye shall go out with joy …'"

We sat in the dark car for a while and found some comfort in each other's company. I let him hold my hand and asked him no more questions. The things we didn't know about each other faded, as the light of day disappeared from the skyline. I took Dakimu back to the hospital and drove home, trying to sing that prophetic song we had heard in St. Joseph's sanctuary, at the turning point of our lives.

Jim and Reena moved into the Imperial Arms the next day. Dakimu said he had friends to stay with, but I knew he was just giving the Stones some time alone. What I didn't know was that he met Father Amani every day for the next week. He had come by the hospital looking for me but missed my shift once because I traded with someone, and another time because I had gone home early with a headache. Personally, I thought it more a heartache but couldn't tell my supervisor that. Finally, I went to the Imperial Arms, and he was there with Jim and Reena. They each hugged me, Dakimu a bit tighter.

He whispered in my ear, "I have missed you."

"I am happy to see you … all."

Jim grabbed my hands. "Please stay in our lives, dear lady," he said.

Do you mean Dakimu's? I thought, but that was unfair. I could not know the darkest or the brightest corners of their hearts or what they had been through as friends. Then Jim handed me a red leather book with the title in gold lettering: *Memoirs on an African Morning.*

"Dakimu has allowed me to give you this story. It is ours. It tore us apart and brought us together. And perhaps a part of it has remained unwritten."

"You wrote it?" I asked him.

"Yes, many years ago. But it is now a piece of Dakimu's present journey."

That's when I learned he had been seeing Father Amani, who was attempting to find the families Dakimu had hurt I knew not how. The book would tell me.

"I want you to read it, Reena, so you can understand everything and walk away if you have to," Dakimu said.

"If Father Amani can trust you, so can I," I said in a rush.

"I hope so … Just read it, and then we'll talk."

I could not put the book down. These people had held each other's lives in their hands, had been terrified of each other and loved each other fiercely, had questioned their most irrational feelings about race and about

God. Their names were not in the book, but Reena and Dakimu leaped off the pages and into the light of the history of Tanzania, no amount of subtle words could hide.

But the hardest things to read were the accounts of Dakimu killing whites and Christian blacks and even children during the Massacre, that he had vowed allegiance to King Kisasi and denied the Christ he had loved. His present remorse seemed meager compensation for such terrible acts. But he was so hungry for redemption. Seeking a priest seemed a cry of desperation.

How could I stand by him? Oh, I knew very well what he needed, and against my nature, I desired to give it—forgiveness, strength, and love. So I began meeting him outside the cathedral, sitting in the serene sanctuary, studying the lessons Father Amani asked him to learn for his first Communion. Reena and Jim had promised to be there for that, but the closer it came to that day, the more wary Dakimu became, not just of his religious conversion but of the events that were culminating outside the church.

"Reena ... it's getting dangerous for me to be so openly looking for my enemies, the sons and daughters of the people I killed. Some say I should leave Dar es Salaam and run for my life, but if I run, I will never have any peace. I wish you would not be so reckless and run yourself, from me, from those who hate me, from my conflicts about the Church. I'm not sure I can go all the way with this. This Communion you wish me to have feels like a death sentence."

"It is a life sentence, Dakimu," I said.

"I want it, but I am afraid of it," he said, and then he spoke a line he had learned long before his talks with Father Amani. "'He who saves his life shall lose it; he who loses his life shall save it.' I understand that now, finally."

"Dak ... if you want to run, I'll go with you," I said, surprising myself.

"Oh, no, dear girl, I could not disrupt your life like that."

We were lingering in the dim sanctuary, the latest in the afternoon we had been there, and I took his face in my hands and pulled him close enough to kiss. He did the rest, putting his mouth gently on mine and then more deeply, offering me his soul, without a thought of Reena Pavane.

"Are you sure about this, Reena?" he asked, after he broke away.

"As sure as I've ever been about anything," I answered, and he held me until the church was dark and the night man came around to lock the doors.

Days passed into weeks and then months. No one talked about returning to Huzuni. Jim and Reena's rooms at the Imperial Arms felt like a safe place. No one was interested in two white people and so never expected Dakimu to be there. I spent more hours there than at my home. Dak and I didn't make love at first, even though the Stones gave us plenty of time alone. We would slowly remove articles of clothing and claim each part of the other's body for our own, not as a possession but as a gift.

It was good that I was there so often, because sometimes in passing I noticed Jim failing a bit and brought varying doses of his medicine back from Dr. Mbulu. We all depended on each other and grew close. I was loved by three amazing people, who completely revolutionized my idea about whites. Without Dak, that might never have happened. They included me in everything, but I knew I was still somehow *outside* and that they would protect each other at all costs. I could only love Dakimu and dream of the rest—being with him, and Reena and Jim, forever.

I was so unprepared for what I would do, if decisions were left in my hands. I believed in God's law and loved a man at odds with that law, who was trying to find it and obey it again. Dakimu and I progressed to very ungodly sex, while later he and I sat demurely in front of the priest, immersed in Catechism. Oh, the irony of our intent!

One night, Dakimu told me about John Sommers, a British officer that he had worked for in the fifties, but killed in 1961. The man's son was in Dar es Salaam, seeking answers about his father's murder. The trail was leading to Dakimu, and though he was longing to express his sorrow to the man, he had heard the man was out for undeniable revenge. Father Amani said Dak should face him, but he couldn't do it yet.

First, Dakimu wanted the Communion promised by our priest. So on a gray-skied afternoon, we all knelt in the cathedral in the presence of Father

Amani. Only Dakimu would receive the body and the blood of Christ, having finished to Father's satisfaction his Catechism. I elected to be only a witness. I could not get that anthem out of my mind. "Ho, everyone that thirsteth … come ye to the waters," and Dak's saying, "The sacred can kill you."

Father Amani blessed the bread and the wine and intoned the litany in Latin at Dak's request. *"Kyrie eleison … Christe eleison."* Dak responded at the appropriate places. I was so moved, a killer at the feet of God, an assassin in the most holy sanctuary in the city.

Dakimu made the sign of the cross for the first time, and I thought, *finally he is in this, cut off from Reena.* She hugged him, and I could tell he acknowledged the split, but he hesitated to let go of her.

Jim hugged him, too, and said, "Much peace to you, my dear friend."

"The days of unrest are still to come," Dak replied.

We went back to the Imperial Arms about nine o'clock in the evening and had a small meal. We spoke very little, but then Reena dared to ask, "Will you meet David Sommers now?"

"I suppose," Dak said, "but I must not put any of you at risk."

"We can't lose you, Dakimu," Jim said. "You are worth any risk imaginable. Will you stay close tonight?"

"I will … but I want to take Reena up to the Point. It's lovely at night. We may be a few hours."

"All right … but be careful," Jim said.

"Hm … God will care for me, if He will," Dak said solemnly.

We left them at the table and took my car up the twisting, hill-hugging road out of Dar es Salaam to a high place overlooking the city and the dark Indian Ocean below. It was almost midnight by then, but we were empowered by the events of the day.

"The haven of peace," Dak said, spreading his hands out over the magnificent view, translating its name with some irony in his voice.

No sooner had he spoken these words than we heard the sound of tires on the gravel road. A truck was speeding up behind us, skidding to a halt, and two white men scrambled out. They had guns.

"Oh, God," Dak cried and lifted me over to the back seat and commanded me to stay down.

I was wild with fear, but it was over before I could think straight. Dak fired a rifle he had retrieved from under the front seat that he admitted to me later had been concealed there for weeks.

I screamed.

"Reena, just don't move. Don't look out."

He swerved the car around and headed downhill. He wouldn't let me get up until we were weaving our way through the streets of Dar es Salaam back to the Imperial Arms. He asked me then to spend the rest of the night with Jim and Reena, and he hurried away. I climbed the stairs to their apartment. I felt faint. Dakimu had not even said where he was going. Jim opened the door.

"Reena ... where's Dak?"

"I don't know ... something terrible happened ... up at the Point. There were two white men ... gunshots, but we escaped harm. I think Dakimu might have killed them. That's all I know."

By then, Reena was there and led me to a chair. I was shaking and trying not to cry.

"Dak was so afraid of this," she said. "Some people will never forgive, mostly the white people. Listen, Reena, did you see anything?"

"No," I answered, wondering if I did but had blocked it out.

"Then this is what we'll say. It's simple. You and Dak were here with us from nine until ... what time is it now? Two a.m. ... until two a.m."

"I don't know," I said. The lie seemed wrong.

"We must do this, Reena," she said. "For Dak. He has suffered enough."

"He has suffered because you couldn't love him!" I blurted out.

"Then that is why I will lie for him," she said calmly and without reproach.

"But I have no reason to ... I have never lied," I said, trying to match her calmness.

"He became a Catholic for you. That must mean something."

"No ... he became a Catholic for himself!"

"Do you love him?" she asked, still calm.

"I do ... but I am so small a part of his life. These things he and you have been through are so big. I do not fit," I said.

"You fit the minute we walked into your hospital, you with my name, I with your mother's salvation, and a black man to capture your heart. You fit all right," she admonished me.

"I want to fit ... more than anything," I said.

"Then you will lie," she said with assurance, then shook her head and said, "No. You must follow your heart."

Jim was just hanging up the phone.

"He's with Father Amani ... he won't say where. I don't think St. Joseph's."

"Father knows how to hide people," I told them.

Jim went on, "Amani wants him to turn himself in and trust the law. It is his country. Who will care about two white men with guns? But we must still say Dakimu and you were here. It's the only guarantee."

"I was taught not to lie," I said.

"I have seen the truth devastate lives," Jim said.

"Maybe those men are still alive," I said hopefully.

"I doubt that," Jim said, shaking his head. "I believe it was your lives or theirs."

"Oh, God, you're right. He was saving *me*! Of course I must lie to save *him*!"

"Then it's agreed."

"It's agreed."

At first light on Sunday morning, one black and two white policemen knocked on the door.

"We have a warrant to search for Dakimu Reiman," they said.

"Search all you want," Jim said. "He's not here. He left early for church."

"When did you last see him?" they questioned.

"Just an hour ago," Reena answered. "He was here all night. Why?"

"Police business. We'll find him."

"What has he done?"

The black officer said in a low voice, as he was the last out, "He killed two white men up at the Point around midnight."

"That's impossible," Jim said. "He was right here with us. We talked until two a.m. I'm not sure when he left this morning or if he went out and came back to get ready for Mass. As my wife said, she saw him an hour ago."

"I'll remember that," the black man said.

Then he looked at me. "Are you his girlfriend?"

"Yes," I said.

"Tell him to give himself up … if he is so innocent." And then he was gone.

The day wore on. I missed my shift at the hospital. Apparently the officers showed up there to interrogate me further. We all jumped when the phone rang. Friends from Huzuni called to ask about Jim and Dak. A parishioner from St. Joseph's called to invite Reena to Catechism class. Dr. Mbulu called with a new prescription for Jim.

Jim said, "There's no prescription for what ails me now."

Finally, Father Amani called and asked for me. I grabbed the receiver.

"I have taken Dakimu to the police station. They will allow him one visitor. He wants you," he said, some tension in his voice.

He wants me! I would go to him. More importantly, I would have the chance to tell him about our lie. Father Amani said Dak had refused to speak, and Father had to ask the police why they were harassing Dakimu's friends. They acted totally oblivious to the priest's entreaties.

We rushed downtown, and I was shown to a small, bare room where Dakimu sat with hands and legs shackled. They wouldn't let me touch him, but I quickly reminded him of the pleasant evening we had spent with Jim and Reena and how we were all together until at least two a.m.

He nodded with sudden understanding and then said, "I love you, Reena Pavane," and I knew he meant me.

A trial date was set. No one believed our story. My tire tracks were the only ones found at the scene that were fresh that night. They assumed I would not have gone up there alone. Father Amani was able to see Dak, and he related everything he could about Dak's physical and emotional state. We heard that some blacks from out of town had been called as witnesses for the prosecution, and we couldn't figure out who they might be. What blacks would testify against him?

I didn't go home at all but stayed with Jim and Reena between shifts. They shared more stories about their friendship with Dak and tried to prepare me for the lie. I went to Father Amani.

He said, "God will forgive your choice, either way."

But my whole being was in turmoil. I was now so far beyond the safety net I had created for myself, I couldn't see any way back. I felt trapped, and then I chided myself for thinking that when Dakimu was the one in the cell.

The day of the trial was hot and stormy. The courtroom was overflowing. We sat near the front, as we were the first to speak for the defense. Dakimu was brought in, still in chains, but he looked at us with such love, it silenced the room.

We were called one at a time, after Dakimu stated that he had been with us most of the night, for sure during the hour the murders were committed.

Jim had no problem saying that was true, and Reena was more specific.

"He was at my home at nine o'clock for dinner and did not leave until two a.m. the next morning."

People murmured in disbelief. Why would these white Americans perjure themselves for this black African?

Then it was my turn.

I could not look at Dak. I loved him, but the lie faltered on my lips. I told the court what happened, that I had been shoved to the back seat and didn't see anything, up on the Point at midnight with Dakimu Reiman.

There was chaos in the courtroom, then chaos in my heart. What had I done to him? I still could not look at him when I passed by, but he made sure I heard his voice.

"There was nothing else you could do. You followed your heart to me and followed your heart to the truth."

And then to Reena and Jim, who had leaned forward in their seats, "Justice, for me, may show another face."

And at that moment, a striking young black man broke through the crowd and through the cordon of guards to stand before Dakimu, who now had his head in his hands. Their likeness was stunning. Dak turned his eyes toward the sound of the young man's voice, consuming the space around the prisoner, drowning out the multitude of voices, drawing a magnificent light upon the face of the condemned Dakimu.

The young man said, "I am your son."

A New Heaven and a New Earth

◇ ◆ ◇

When I looked up at Dakimu and saw the young African reaching out to him, I was flung back to the wet and crumbling shore of the Rufiji River and the half-dead black man in my arms! The boy had the face of that distant black and now his voice, as I heard him say, "I am your son."

The crowd was in chaos, the judge banging his gavel and crying for silence. But above the din, I heard the word *son*! Dakimu grabbed his hands for a moment before the guards pulled them apart and threw the young man to a chair a few rows back. I got up and went to him, touching his shoulder.

The first words he said to me were, "Is this what your love has done?"

And then Jim reached out for both of us, as Dakimu was dragged out of the courtroom, begging to be able to speak to the boy.

"Stay by us," Jim was saying. "We'll help you."

"My mother ..." the young man began, pointing toward a place in the crowd but apparently not recognizing anyone there.

"I'll find her," I said. "What does she look like?"

"She is a thin African woman wearing a long dress of blues and gold and is carrying a red leather-bound book, *your* book!" he said staring at Jim.

Jim would not let go of the boy, even though a uniformed man approached with handcuffs.

"He's done nothing wrong!" Jim cried. "Leave him with me. There'll be no trouble."

I was pushing my way through the gathering, trying to see the colors on the boy's mother. When I finally got outside, I noticed a woman moving in slow circles on the courthouse lawn. There was a flash of red in her hand. I moved carefully, not wanting to scare her.

"Mother?" I said in Swahili.

She finally found my eyes, held out the red volume, and said, "Book ... book," with a veiled desperation.

"Let me show you," I said, and I turned to the pages where it described how Jim had lifted me into the helicopter and taken me away from Huzuni with the Vitani closing in around us. The book had been translated into her language. I read a few paragraphs. She nodded her head, and then I put my hand on my heart and said, "Reena Pavane ... I am Reena Pavane ... I am *that* girl."

She let me take her hand and reenter the courthouse. Jim still had one arm around the beautiful young black.

"Kiiku!" the mother said joyfully.

He told her in Swahili that the man at his side had written her treasured red book. But she knew Jim. She spoke to him about things that happened over twenty-five years ago. She put her hands on his face.

"Good friend ... good friend," she said haltingly.

"Who are you?" Jim asked.

"Kisasi ... daughter," she answered.

The boy spoke with pride, "My grandfather!" and took his mother's hand.

"King Kisasi," Jim whispered.

"I haven't read the book," Kiiku said, "but I've always known about my father. I must see him!"

"Young man, we'll do whatever we can. Let's try to find the judge," Jim said.

We all walked down a long hall, absent now of spectators. Kiiku's mother clung to her son but held back in some discomfort, seeming to understand that he was going to see his father. Jim and I stayed a little way behind. Dakimu's Reena had disappeared in the confusion. The trial wasn't really over, and she would be called back. We decided she had probably gone to St. Joseph's and was with Father Amani. We didn't know if he'd been in the courtroom. Of course, he knew more of the truth than any of us but could never break the confidence of his parishioner.

The judge had called a recess when Reena broke down on the witness stand and Kiiku struggled to his father's side. It was such a tumultuous moment. There were so many unanswered questions. The look on Dak's face broke my heart. He loved Reena and had to accept that she loved the truth more. He forgave her instantly, which made the appearance of his son seem a gift from the hand of God.

We stood at the judge's door, two whites and two blacks seeking more than justice. The door opened, and a court officer allowed us in. The judge was hanging up his robe. He did not look happy.

"What is the meaning of this?" he asked brusquely.

Who should speak?

Kiiku dropped his mother's hand, bowed slightly toward the magistrate, and said, "Sir ... that man you have taken away is my father. This is the first time I have seen him in my life. I only want to talk to him, to look into his eyes ... nothing more."

"We don't let murderers have visitors," the judge said matter-of-factly.

"It has not been proven yet," Kiiku said. "What if the girl lied?"

"What if those white people lied?" he said, pointing at Jim and me.

"I don't care ... I love my father. I need to see him. I implore you."

"I suppose *you* are the most innocent in all this," the judge said.

He spoke to his officer. "Bring the prisoner to my chambers and clear the others from the room."

Kiiku let out a deep breath and then spoke softly to his mother. "I believe you are safe with these white people. You seem to remember Jim Stone. I don't know why, but will you go out with him?"

She nodded and moved closer to Jim. We went reluctantly into the hall and sat on a hard bench by a small window that showed the narrow and cluttered streets of Dar es Salaam. I only know what was said between

Dak and his son because it was recorded, and I was able to get the tape, thanks to Father Amani. The judge was a Catholic and was softened by the priest's pleas.

✛   ✛   ✛

There was a long silence in the beginning of the tape. It was hard to tell if they were touching, but finally Dakimu said,

"I did not know about you."

"You knew about my sister," Kiiku says.

"She was not mine," Dak replies with a sigh.

"I figured that out. I was her friend though, till the end."

"The end?"

"She died many years ago."

"I'm sorry ... I'm truly sorry. Your mother could not have been much comfort."

"She told me about you ... 'a bad man,' she said a hundred times. But I didn't want to believe it."

"And what do you believe now?" Dak asks.

"You are a bad man ... but you are my father. I must listen to your story."

"I don't think we have that much time, my son."

"Should I read the red book?" Kiiku asks.

Again, silence.

"It will tell you a lot ... but not everything," Dak says softly.

"Do you love the white people?"

"Jim and Reena? Yes, very much."

"Did you love my mother?"

"No, son, I could not. I married her to save the white man."

"Oh," Kiiku says.

"It's complicated ... but know that I would never have abandoned you!" Dak says with great emotion.

"You were gone when I was born."

"I had promises to keep," Dak tells his son.

"Will you promise me something?"

"Anything."

"Will you be my father?" Kiiku asks in a choked voice.

"If justice allows it," Dak says.

"Tell me their names again ... the white people," Kiiku says.

"Jim and Reena Stone. I married them several months ago and a few hours later met a black woman named after her, the Reena Pavane who was last on the stand."

"She betrayed you!" Kiiku cries.

"No, son. She is a lover of truth."

"Is she your lover, too?"

"Yes."

"Do you know where she went?"

"I think so ... to St. Joseph's Cathedral."

"She's Catholic?"

"Yes ... as am I," Dakimu says softly.

"Do you want me to befriend her?"

"Would you?"

"I would do anything for you ... I have so many years to amend our relationship."

"No, my son, that is my job."

A door opened, and the chains on Dakimu's legs could be heard scraping the floor.

"Father ..." Kiiku calls out.

"I will pray that we will be together again, son."

And he was gone.

✢   ✢   ✢

When Kiiku came out of the judge's chambers, his heart seemed irretrievable. We were strangers, after all. Even his own mother was lost to him, mumbling to herself and turning in erratic circles.

I was the first to speak. "Kiiku ... what can we do?"

"I don't know ... I just can't lose my father now after wanting him, dreaming of him, my whole life, being separated from him for so many years."

"Jim and I were separated from Dak for many years, too. But he was always in our hearts, and in some way, perhaps you were in our hearts," I said.

That broke the ice. Kiiku took Jim's hand and then embraced me shyly.

"Anyone my father loves should have my good will," he said. "I'm going to take my mother home. I will not let her testify. She could hurt my father without even realizing it. I'll tell the court she became ill. Everyone could see she was confused."

"Will you come back to us?" Jim asked.

"Yes … I must find my father's friend Reena. It was the only thing he asked of me, and to learn more about you."

"We're at the Imperial Arms. We'll be waiting for you," Jim said, letting go of his hand reluctantly.

And we parted in the late afternoon, so many pieces of the puzzle still missing, still locked inside each heart. We hated to see them go. Kiiku's mother had a piece of the puzzle we would never know, she being incapable of sharing it, and we perhaps being incapable of understanding it.

Jim and I looked at each other with constrained joy. Dak had a son, a wonderful young man he may never really know. And with Reena, so much possible love and fulfillment for him riding on the edge of redemption. Could Africa ever heal the wounds we all had borne? Could God?

With that thought in mind, we drove to St. Joseph's. The cathedral's stained glass glimmered in the bright rays of the equatorial sun, a sign of hope. Father Amani met us on the steps.

"Reena is here … but I don't think you should see her," he said.

"But, Father, we have only good things to tell her. Dak had some time with his son. And he asked Kiiku to find her," I said.

"Come with me," he said.

Reena was in the priest's private quarters. She was sitting so still she almost didn't look real. She didn't meet our eyes.

"Reena, you had no choice," I began. "You had to tell the truth."

"No … I should have lied for him. I love him."

"Love does not require you to lie," I said.

"You and Jim did!" she accused.

"Well … yes." I couldn't argue with her.

"What happened … with that young man?" she asked.

"He was brought here with his mother," Jim hesitated, "to testify against him. We don't know what she would have said, but she was clearly … incompetent. The boy begged to see his father, and he and Dak had about fifteen minutes together. His name is Kiiku, and he has been longing for his father his whole life. His mother seems obsessed with *Memoirs*, and she remembers me being in the Vitani encampment! I don't remember her, but I was delirious half the time, in a dark hut. I never saw her outside. Some of the women hid themselves from me, afraid of my white skin or maybe my camera. I can't imagine Dak … with her, but here is that sweet boy with nothing but love in his heart for a man he never knew. Dak asked him to find you."

"Oh, no," Reena cried.

"It will be a few days, I think. He took his mother home," I added.

"What can I say to him?" she asked.

"Just tell him you love his father," Jim offered.

"I'll tell him what happened! I know those white men would have killed us up at the Point! Dak can't go to prison for saving my life!"

"Come home with us, Reena," I said. "We'll figure something out."

"Why couldn't I just tell the lie?" she stammered.

"Because it's not who you are," I answered.

Later that night, we sat on the couch with the calming view of the Indian Ocean, its luscious turquoise almost black under a moonless sky. Reena was very quiet. She let me fix her a cup of tea but wouldn't eat the sandwiches I made for us. She was close to tears many times but was immune to our comfort.

Then our lives were turned upside down when Kiiku showed up past midnight. He was out of breath and excited.

"I know what we have to do," he started in without really looking at any of us.

The door still stood open, and a stormy wind slammed it against the inside wall of the apartment. Jim closed it and grasped Kiiku's arm.

"Kiiku, calm down. Everything is okay for now," he said.

"Okay? How can you say that? Two white people lied under oath for my father, and his black lover sent him to jail with the truth! I have spent my life hearing the gruesome details of the life of the father I loved! It is not okay!"

"Sit down, Kiiku," Jim commanded. "Don't you know how special you are to us? We will do anything for you and your father. His suffering is our suffering ... and always has been. We'll be there for him now."

"I'm not talking about standing up for him or lying or praying! I'm talking about breaking him out!"

We were stunned. He had driven many hours burning with this plan, thinking we would agree to it and help him. But isn't that exactly what we did in New York? Help Dak escape from the band of law enforcement tightening around him for the murders of Hahlos and Old George?

So I said, "Kiiku ... do you realize that's how he got back to Africa twenty years ago? Jim and I broke him out of the city where he faced certain execution. I don't think he'll let us do that again."

"I brought people back with me who know how to do it!" he admitted.

"Kiiku, your father would not want you to break the law," I said.

"Because he's Catholic now?"

"For many reasons ..."

"I'm going to reclaim those years I lost!" he said defiantly.

"Maybe you will get them in a way you least expect," I suggested.

He sat down then and looked at Reena. She was curled in an odd shape in one corner of the couch.

"And what do you have to say for yourself?" he asked in a harsh voice.

"I love him," she said.

"A lot of good it did," he said, still angry.

Reena said, meeting his eyes finally, "He killed those men for me! That's what I wanted to say on the stand. Those white men were running toward our car with guns! They wanted your father, but they surely wouldn't have left a witness. I am so sorry, Kiiku."

No one spoke for a while. I was just glad Kiiku had come back to us. He must have raced down the dusty roads and winding canyons to get here so fast. We had to protect him from his pain at finding his father locked up, after imagining this reunion for so long.

"I don't know any white people," he said at last. "I've been taught not to trust them. But when you lied for my father, that did something to me. Right there in the courtroom, I felt a shock. Such friendship is beyond my experience."

I smiled. "I was much younger than you when I met your father, but the friendship came almost at once and remained through very difficult times. You could learn more from Jim's book."

"The few lines I read angered me," he said.

"Yes, there is much to make one angry. But there is much that can heal."

He looked tired suddenly, and he dropped his head.

"Kiiku, you have traveled many miles today, in your body and in your mind," Jim said gently. "Will you stay with us and forget this break-out idea?"

"I'll stay ... but I need to free my father."

Reena had gone into the room that had become hers and Dak's and came out with her backpack slung over her shoulder.

"I have to go to work. Kiiku can sleep in my bed. I'll go to my place. I'll be all right."

"Reena ..." Jim started.

"I know you guys care about me. But you have loved Dakimu forever, and now his son is part of your lives. Your path is clear ... mine—not so much."

And she went out the door.

The next morning, I called Father Amani.

He said, "I have something you should hear."

Jim wanted to stay with Kiiku, so I drove alone to the cathedral. The priest handed me the tape from Dak's meeting with his son.

"I don't think this is betraying anyone," he said. "They knew they were being recorded. Please use this wisely."

"Thank you, Father."

I sat in the soft morning light of St. Joseph's sanctuary and played the short tape. "I married her to save the white man." That's what resounded in my head when I turned the recorder off. Dak married Kisasi's slow-witted daughter, and then she had a child by another man. So when he discovered that, he ... *oh God, no.* I couldn't imagine it! But his son was conceived, and the woman never told him! A just revenge, if you can believe she could devise such a thing.

I pictured again the day Dakimu and I lay exhausted on the flood-damaged bank of the Rufiji. How innocent we had been then, how young and full of hope. And what pain and betrayal transpired after that. Maybe Kiiku's plan was best after all. Set Dak free to be a warrior father to the son he never knew and answer to the calling of the drums. How Catholic is he not to want this chance for a new life?

What should I do with this knowledge? Why had Dak never told us about Kisasi's daughter? But I knew the answer. He had told us very little about those days during the Massacre. Those details went into Father Amani's ear. Jim and I knew they were terrible words, admitting to terrible acts. Dak may have believed that God forgave him, but he was not sure we could, so he kept silent about many things. The presence of his son would bring it all to light.

Light. It was beginning to fade, storm clouds gathering over Dar es Salaam, the Indian Ocean in the distance cobbled with white caps, as I stepped out of the cathedral and looked toward the eastern coast of Africa. I had to see Dak. He had called me *his Africa* once, but he was my Africa. I would not reject Kiiku's plan so easily. Dak in prison was something I could not bear.

The guards were suspicious. I lied and said I had permission to visit the prisoner. They opened the gate and let me into his cell. He was lying on a hard bunk with his back to me. I put my hand on his shoulder, and he said, "Reena," before he even turned over.

"Yes, my friend ... I'm here."

He sat up and took both my hands in his. The guards didn't seem to care. He was not as troubled as I had supposed he would be. I noticed a Bible open on a small nightstand.

"It's the one thing they let me have. The judge is Catholic," he said.

"I know," I said.

I hesitated then. I really wanted him to tell me himself, about Kiiku's mother, about the daughter that was not his who died, about the rage that led to Kiiku's conception. How could I set him free, if he wouldn't tell me these things?

"Kiiku?" he said.

"He's with us, Dak."

"I have to tell you something, my dear Reena. I should have told you long ago, you … and Jim. It was always something I could hold on to that was mine alone, a kind of secret that gave me power."

He let go of my hands but kept his eyes on mine when he said, "I married King Kisasi's daughter so he would release Jim from the camp of the Vitani. I saved Jim for you. That was the price I paid."

"Is there more?" I asked.

He shook his head. "If I must tell more and lose your love, it is too high a price."

"I will always love you, Dak."

He raised one hand like a warning and said, "My son, my beautiful Kiiku … is a child of rape. Now … I have everything … and nothing," he cried in the stiffling, bare room.

I did the only thing I could do. I took his face in my hands and gave him what he had always wanted, what he wanted on the dark side of the Rufiji River, what he wanted by the crystal pool deep in the African hills, what he wanted in my apartment in New York. I gave him *that kiss*. And I didn't stop kissing him until the guards wrenched us apart and escorted me roughly to the jailhouse door. One officer grabbed Dak's Bible, slammed it shut shouting, "No more privileges for you!" and threw it at me. I jammed it in my handbag and ran to my car.

As soon as I walked into the apartment, I said to Kiiku, "Get him out … he needs to be out! But Kiiku, do not ever tell us where you have taken him, where you are. This is the price we must pay … to give him a life with you."

He didn't say a word—just turned and disappeared. Jim and I waited until we heard the news that the suspected murderer of two prominent white citizens had been broken out of his cell by a gang of natives unknown in the city.

Jim said, "We didn't say good-bye."

And I replied, "But I think he did."

And we sat down on the couch before the big window, where we had stared at the Indian Ocean, enigmatic as our meeting, without touching but wanting to touch, so many years ago. We looked out now, arm in arm, with the lights of Dar es Salaam beginning to gleam and the sea darker than it had ever been, a cobalt lens unbreakable and serene, a talisman of our union black with white and our letting go. We opened Dakimu's Bible to the place where the marker lay and read together the words his pencil had lined:

> *And I saw a new heaven and a new earth; for the first heaven and the first earth had passed away, and the sea was no more.*
>
> —Revelation 21:1